War and Sexual Adventure in Isis

The story of war, crime, sex slave women and child suicide bombers

By : Amirreza Porhelm

Title: War and Sexual Adventure in Isis

Author: Amirreza Porhelm

ISBN: 9781939123091

Publisher: Supreme Century, Los Angeles, USA

Prepare for Publishing: Asan Nashr
www.ASANASHR.com

Titles

About the Book and Author

He has written numerous books. Those who have read his writings Some say that the prophesied events Including:

America's invasion of Iraq

The arrest of Saddam

Election unrest in Iran in 2009

This book is the story Love Religious Sexual relations and collective Women who provide sexual services to the military Alongside Adventures of a bloody war And children who blew themselves with bombs
The author has begun story Rebellion to hell
Everything starts from there
Now
Start a story

1

Battle in hell

There was a serious battle in the fifth circle of inferno.
The babel of voices could be heard everywhere. The
hellish people were in extreme pain because of their
sins torments. Amongst them, there was a rebel
fighter who had committed terrible crimes in a war in
Middle East a thousand years ago and he was
escaping from a detestable asp snake. He arrived by a
lake of lava, the rebel fighter had two options:
jumping in the lake of fire or being swallowed by the
snake and he didn't have more time to decide.   Angel
of Doom was passing when he saw the disparate and
fearful face of the fighter who was looking for a way
out. Angel of Doom who was used to watching such
scenes pointed to the Lake of lava which meant he
had to choose that. The rebel fell on the ground
hopelessly and said something unclearly. Suddenly

angel of doom   was commanded to put the desperate man on his wings and carry him away. Angel of doom reached the man at the exact moment when the asp snake was going to swallow him.

On the way while angel was flying on top of the lake of lava, he asked the man: "what did you say that you were saved?"

The hellish man was silent and it was like that there was a lock on his mouth, he wasn't able to talk. The angel continued his way for about 300 years of the earth time which only seemed some minutes in hell time. When the Angel reached near the earth, he asked for a command and he was told to land near a place where the most agony had passed to its brute people in past.

The hellish man was left unconscious on the sands of a vast desert.   Angel was forbidden to look at any point on the earth to prevent torments for that place. But as soon as he left the evil fighter on the earth and was going to fly, his eyes stood still to a point not far from him. A beautiful city with blue sky and well-constructed buildings.

A voice said: "That is the land of Sham. Why are your eyes wide open?"

The angel said: "they wouldn't be if you didn't want them to be."

The angel flied to hell from the sky of Iraq and disappeared in horizon.

During the night a horrific storm of dust raised. The thunder was like a monster who was yelling in fear. The rebel fighter recognized that monster but he wasn't able to speak.

The rebel in exile could exactly remember the place where he was landed. The city where he had invaded a thousand years ago with his men and had killed all its occupants. This city was near Aleppo, the ancient part of it was buried under thousands tones of dust. And he knew it all.

Memories from a thousand years ago appeared in front of his eyes clearly and his soul on the earth was feeling that the fight at this place has just happened some days ago. He remembered when he ordered to kill all of the men of a village and keep the women for pleasure. The rebel leader remembered when he decided to behead a man in front of his family. Then in a moment he noticed that his child is looking at him, suddenly something shook his heart and he ordered to leave that family.

While the hellish man was on the ground he started to talk and whispered: "Damn you the land of unmerciful tyrants! Damn the foundations of your land from where you sent the leaders to the depth of hell and recalled them from fire! Damn you!"

2

The evils' meeting

In the evening of a February night 2004, a bus carrying some dangerous terrorists stopped next to a prison in Basra. The American troops had blindfolded the prisoners. "These assholes weren't comfortable in Abu Ghraib" A fat American soldier said to the one in charge of receiving the prisoners. "But I'm sure they're gonna have fun here!"

"terrorists?" the female American soldier in charge of receiving prisoners asked.

The fat soldier admitted with a nod of the head while inhaling his cigarette smoke. "If I were you I would have dropped some deadly scorpions inside their cell." he said.

"Doing such a folly, we're gonna end up in the jail. It's better to wait until they are released and government offers a reward for their head," the female soldier replied.

The American soldiers thought the terrorists were bunch of idiots who don't understand their language, but Abu Bakr could realize what they were saying.

"Who is Abu Bakr?" the female soldier asked while looking at the information papers.

A prisoner raised his hand without saying a word.

"Are you sure he is not here by a mistake? He is a professor," the woman said to her colleague.

"He is a murderer," the fat soldier answered indifferently.

The prisoners went to their cell which was a cozy four-bed dormitory room. "We must start from here!" Abu Muslim one of Abu Bakr's comrades said.

"I am going to start sending mails tomorrow. There are guys out there waiting for my orders." Abu Bakr said.

Gradually this evil group got the control of the prison. The Americans were just guarding outside the prison and they had nothing to do with inside. Abu Muslim identified some prisoners who didn't pray. He reported to Abu Bakr and they planned to send them to hell.

The Arab jihadis in Iraq received the letters from Abu Bakr with this message: "Ruin the walls!"

Bombings and explosions increased in Iraq but no one could imagine the massacres were led by somebody inside the prison.

The prison was full of professional Arab murderers. They could easily contact each other and a network had been built inside the prison which connected them. They had insane plans for the days of freedom.

Abu Bakr and his friends were released unexpectedly from Basra prison on December that year. Some days later the American authorities of Basra prison noticed that their freedom command was sent by mistake. The US military commander in Iraq noticed later that the release command of some Jihadis from Basra prison should not have included the dangerous ones like Abu Bakr and his men. The Americans had thought that if they released some jihadis who are less dangerous, the anti-American sentiment in Iraq might have been reduced.

Iraqi assassins who knew themselves as jihadis were planning for sabotages. Every night after the Salat of Maghreb they went into tunnels under the ground to plan terrors and explosions.

Abu Bakr talked for them about the rewards for killing and insisted that assassinating each kafir would make a way to paradise for them. One of their main plans was to make an insecure and horrifying atmosphere in Baghdad.

Baghdad seemed the most disordered city in the world. Blood and prejudice ruled in all districts of the city. There was a ridiculous satanic situation. Every morning mangled bloody corpses of some person with no name were found in large waste containers or in potholes on passages. Sometimes heads were put on fencings of houses or stores which made horror to anyone who passed by them in the middle of the night or early in the morning. The victims' main crime was to have another religion and other beliefs.

Terror squads were active all over Iraq. Just a little bad luck was enough to enter a name in the terror black list. Abu Bakr al-Baghdadi replaced Abu Musab al-Zarqawi the leader of al-Qaeda in Iraq. Al-Zarqawi and al-Baghdadi both were specialists in massacre and bloodshed. No criminal could be found even in the worst New York districts who was skilled in killing like them.

Abu Bakr and his men spread terror and insecurity in a way that everyone thought it is the remaining of Saddam system just making troubles. Ayman al-Zawahiri the, al-Qaeda leader was constantly in contact with Baghdadi. Al-Zawahiri was an old idiot with no specific strategy.

"How does the massacre go in Iraq? Can we be hopeful to purge Iraq from kafirs before long?" once he asked al-Baghdadi.

"We are killing continuously." Al-Baghdadi replied, "Bloodshed has become ordinary. We may destroy the whole country and leave no one."

Al-Zawahiri believed his disgusting joke."Are you out of your mind?" he said, We want an insecure Iraq for kafirs. Just kill Americans and Shiites. I have been reported that a magnificent castle is being made for you in heaven. The more you kill, the sooner the materials would be there."

Abu Bakr intensified the insane massacre in Iraq. He even once attached a bomb which he had always with himself to a car, a woman's car who had brought her child from school and Abu Bakr did it just for fun. The attaching bombs explode within 30 seconds of attachment letting nothing to remain. Then he stared at the scene insanely while laughing and showing his disgusting teeth.

The United States Central Command in Iraq received reports demonstrating that Abu Bakr al-Baghdadi was planning terrorist attacks in a safe house in Baqubah. The report was complete and accurate. The Americans managed an unmanned aerial vehicle to bomb his residence. Abu Bakr was watching TV with one of his men named Abu Hajar. There was a Kalashnikov by his side leaned on the wall. He started swearing to Americans. Abu Hajar was cooking chicken on the fire. Abu Bakr was holding a paper and pen in his hand and he was writing down every name coming to his mind. He was making a 100 person list of people whom he considered kafir and najis. There was eight American commanders and five Iranians in the list who were active in Iraq.

Abu Bakr was leaving the room for Wudu when he heard the aircraft's voice. Abu Hajar looked at him while holding a piece of chicken and they both rushed to a tunnel which led them to a drainage channel. The American missiles almost ruined that house.

***

In a desert district inside Anbar province in Iraq, near Syria border, there was a huge tent with some armored fighting vehicles, a water tank and Toyota pickup around it. Abu Hajar was cleaning the dirt between his toes when Abu Bakr came and asked him if he was getting ready for Salat.

Abu Hajar replied: "I dreamt of a woman last night and I was making love to her. I had a wet dream, so I'm najis (ritual impure)."

Abu Bakr got angry and kicked him out of the tent. "If you don't perform the ghusl in two minutes, I will cut you into half," he threatened.

Abu Bakr returned to tent. The TV was showing the news about protests in Syria. He gazed at TV for some minutes and something came to his mind.

He put a message in the draft folder of common e-mail with Ayman al-Zawahiri so the old idiot could read and reply it as soon as possible. All jihadi leaders connected to al-Qaeda had a common e-mail with al-Zawahiri with a fake ID. The messages never were sent for security reasons. They knew Americans could track them if they send any messages.

Abu Bakr wrote in his message to al-Zawahiri: "I go to Syria to start a revolution."

Two days later al-Zawahiri replied: "Stay in Iraq, we have men for revolution over there."

Abu Bakr whispered swearwords in response.

Apparently he was going to do his own business.

3

The revolution fever

On a Friday protest in Syria when a crowd of about
two or three thousand people had held anti-
government protest in the city of Aleppo, the street
fighting started with military soldiers' gunfire.
Suddenly anti-riot forces faced masked men who fired
them back with their weapons.

The governmental forces were surprised and they ran
away when some of them fell on the ground.
Apparently only a small attack was enough to make
the soldiers escape. The protesters all screamed with
happiness. There was the scent of Libya in the air. In
coming days some military centers were out of control
of governmental forces. The videos released in social
networks encouraged the armed opponents. The

armed fighters increased gradually and they fought to governmental forces in every protest.

The group led by Abu Bakr al-Baghdadi (Islamic State) was one of the organizations who took the most advantage from the messy situation in Syria. They passed unorganized Iraq border in the middle of the night so easily and entered a village named Al-Hasakah in Syria. Abu Bakr's militants killed men and women in random shooting to horrify people. The whole village were slept in the calm of the night when it was attacked. The children and women were screaming. Abu Bakr's men were laughing loud with their deep Arabic accents.

Militants attacked a village house and broke in the room. The family man came out and he was confused. "What do you Think of Assad?" One of them asked him.

The poor man who thought that he was attacked by the governmental forces replied in fear: "Assad is our master and chief."

This mistake was enough for militants to shoot him and all his family. The village fell so easily and Abu Bakr's army moved ahead to Ar-Raqqah. They arrived in Ar-Raqqah about 3:30 in the morning. Abu Bakr al-Baghdadi insanely ordered to inspect every house at that time.

An Arab militant patrolled in the town with a car and announced using loudspeakers: "We are the Islamic army and we took the town from kafirs. Whoever is faithful and swears allegiance to al-Baghdadi is safe."

No one came out of their houses. Abu Bakr commanded to invade the houses. They pulled every one out of their beds, tied their hands behind their back and blindfolded them. The slept people thought they were having a nightmare and they woke up just when they felt the guns on their head and kicks on their ass.

They brought men out of their houses in groups. Women and children were screaming. They laid tied up men on the ground and kicked on their neck once in a while. They moved people from around the town to a big square. It was the time for Adhan. Abu Bakr had decided to make people swear allegiance in that night.

The men who had shaved their bread were brought to mosques to be whipped. Whoever had a tattoo was pulled out of bed in shorts and took to be whipped. After being whipped they signed a commitment not to shave anymore and clean all the signs on their hands and bodies.

The oath was taken under the force of swords. Abu Bakr was joyful of going back in time for about fourteen centuries. Then he sent a reconnaissence team to investigate the situation around the town. The investigation showed there is nothing around other than corpses and half burnt tanks.

The situation inside the city was extremely messy and disordered. Sunni tribes had sworn allegiance to Jolani who was the chief of al-Nusra, an Islamic violent terrorist group and there was a serious war to occupy the town. The spies reported Jolani that Abu Bakr al-Baghdadi is advancing so fast to other districts of Ar-

Raqqah. Al-Nusra commander got so angry. The city situation was awful. Gunshot and explosion didn't stop even for a second. The governmental army was defending the city. Al-Nusra militants and unsatisfied Sunnis arranged an attack to city government and arrested the state authorities in a shameful way.

Jolani knew so well that Abu Bakr's army is just few kilometers away from him so he strengthen the city entrances. Abu Bakr called his cell phone to inform that his forces were supposed to enter the city. "We have occupied the city son of a bitch." Jolani said, "What the hell do you do here?"

"I will be in the city within an hour and I'll send you and your men straight to the hell. Pray to God that I treat you well," Abu Bakr replied.

Jolani contacted immediately with Ayman al-Zawahiri. The old man of al-Qaeda had felt asleep after reading Quran. The fighter who was guarding outside the cave where he lived told it to Jolani who was insisting to speak to him.

"Wake the old idiot up!" Jolani told him. Al-Zawahiri came to the phone with a sleepy voice. "What is it? Did you capture Damascus?" he said.

"This bitch, Abu Bakr, your man in Iraq has declared war on me and now he wants to push me out of the city where I have occupied by force," Jolani said.

"Give him the city and move forward. He is insane and he has no honor. He has to be in Ar-Raqqah by God commands. Go and occupy other places and raise the flag of Islam," Al-Zawahiri replied.

Jolani finally gave up and gathered his forces and equipment to evacuate the city. In some minutes Abu Bakr's pickups and forces showed up in Ar-Raqqah. They occupied the city with their black flags.

Al-Nusra left Ar-Raqqah completely with their armored vehicles and went to Homs. In a short while the pickups of Abu Bakr equipped with machine guns were inside the city. They had installed the black flag on top of their equipment with the phrase of "La Ilaha Illallah". The normal life went on in Ar-Raqqah. The governmental forces ran away and presented the city to military opponents. The people of Ar-Raqqah didn't know what a dreadful nightmare they were going to have. Abu Bakr ordered militants to go inside the houses, to choose good observation points and to make them their military bases.

Groups of five men were formed. One of these groups moved to fancy houses of Ar-Raqqah. The big houses were quickly occupied by militants. A group of Afghans entered the house and searched every corner of the house. The ex-occupants had almost taken every precious thing. Ahmed the group leader laid on a bed and said: "Sun of a bitch! Look at the beds they slept on!" Then he started daydreaming and addressed one of his comrades who was searching the drawers. "Do you know what is missing on this bed? A beautiful woman who makes me joyful," he said.

"Do you know what is more fun?" One of them said, "To reach a woman while she's naked and she's crying."

The group leader got up angrily. "What the hell are we doing here? Maybe in another house near here a woman is cooking! I wish I can find her in the kitchen," he said.

"I will get close to her slowly from behind and I start to cuddle her. Then I will bite her face." the young militants said.

They moved immediately. They found a woman in the street who was wearing burqa. One of them ordered the woman to stop. She stopped. The leader removed her burqa. It was an old woman with a detestable face. One of the Arabs started a disgusting laughter. They kicked the old woman on the ground.

They moved to a street some blocks further. They chose a house and entered it. The house maid was screaming in fear. The house master was a disabled man whom the woman took care of. Militants tied the handicapped man and took the woman to another room. The men had hairy and fat legs. The woman was horrified but she had no other choice. The attackers were out of their minds. They attacked the woman in group and did what they wanted.

The situation was awful in Ar-Raqqah. Governmental bases fell one after another. Free Syrian Army, al-Nusra and Abu Bakr's Group were in the frontline. Sunnis of each area welcomed them but they regretted soon. In some parts people ran away before the attackers reach there. The runaways went to Turkey and the Turkish government established the Antakya refugee camps.

The border guards of Turkey were ordered to push the refugees back and settle them on the border. There was a camp without any facilities and people lived in tents in big groups.

Some of the girls and women who had beautiful faces were brought to houses of rich people to work. They did the housework and they were also sex partners of the master. Helping the refugees was a good chance for some countries to send armor and weapons to rebel groups of Syria. The boxes of weapons and ammos reached the border of Turkey and Syria between food and drug aid. On the border a Turk General with his men delivered them.

The situation became more and more complicated every day in Syria. Repression of the protests by military was something which made bloodshed something regular. Iran gave riot control weapons and vehicles like water cannons to the Syrians. The experience of confronting riots was transferred by Iranians to security agents in Damascus. Groups of secret police were formed by Assad and assigned to identify the leaders of opponents but it wasn't easy to identify the one on top of all this chaos.

One of the most important security recommendations to Syrian authorities was to arrest the protestors. They had been told that targeted arresting can cause fear and terror between the protesters and prevent them from continuing their protests. The cost of this act was less than massacre. The intelligence and security police came to action. They started severe arrests but it seemed that this issue was not going to end so easily. The protests changed into armed struggles and in this situation intelligence and security methods were not affective anymore.

When al-Nusra and Free Syrian Army were ahead of other groups, sometimes they fought between themselves. After a bloody contention which caused many men of Jolani being killed, the leader of Free Army finally contacted their trusted ones in Ankara and asked about this situation. The subject took eight hours of investigation and during this time more people from both sides were killed. At last a telegraph was received from Turks who insisted that unmarked militants are jihadis who are not to be attacked.

Syrian National Council - who represented Free Syrian Army in politics - was lobbying in different European capitals to be recognized legitimate. Washington had implicitly recognized them legitimate but let them know that they have to do everything by themselves. Because United States, England and NATO had just came out of a crisis in Libya and they had no more money to spend for the subversion of Assad. But the opponents could regularly receive their weapons. The political front of opponents was recognized legitimate by some countries and they were supposed to give them money and weapons through the safe freed areas by militants.

The massive successes just made a big concern: who are the other Islamic militants other than Free Syrian Army? There was a disturbed situation. But Saudis, Turks and Qataris knew who the other militants were.

Tens of rebel Islamic groups controlled different parts of Syria. Providing water and bread by jihadi groups had made an industry with millions of dollars turnover for them which covered a big part of their income.

The rebels kidnapped citizens of other countries in Syria and asked big amounts of money from their families or their governments to free them. The governments usually gave them the money and delivered their citizens in return. But they claimed that they had solved the issue by diplomatic tools in front of public opinion.

Al Nusra and Jolani's group which were acting under the supervision of al-Qaeda, professionally practiced extortion. Their dealing mechanism was like the gangsters. They extracted wealth through taxation and extortion and the money wasn't settled in any bank accounts. They always used regular suitcases full of dollars in their transactions. An expert always checked the bills. Some percent of these extortions was for the head of al-Qaeda and at last al-Zawahiri always wrote a letter with this concept: "Jolani is the good and honorable son of Islam." In this way he used to thank him.

The extortionists had deep holes in the ground to keep the hostages or in some cases they kept the kidnapped person in dirty stables. Their victims were mostly reporters and European tourists. If anyone was caught, he would have experienced the real hell. They had no merci. Plunder and extortion became the developing industry in Syria. They even made legal reasons upon Sharia for their actions. For example they said the hostages were kafirs. Fourteen centuries ago Islam soldiers used to plunder commercial convoys of Quraysh kafirs and use the benefits of selling stolen goods to develop Islam. So their action in the present time is legal.

4

Womanizers

In a cool sunny winter "Penter" the high ranked Saudi intelligent authority was flying to Istanbul with a Qatarian authority. Their personal jet had all facilities. They had sat behind a round table and they were supposed to meet their Turk counterparts in some hours to consult him about supporting armed opponents.

"I really like to put the Iranians in their place. They supported Shiite protesters in Bahrain and made trouble for us. I don't know what they are looking for," Penter told in a mysterious tone.

"Look at them from top, if it was necessary take their tail and throw them out," Qatarian authority said.

Penter laughed ridiculously. "It is so fun to see the coward Iranian faces when they are bringing out Bashar Assad with an underwear from a dark tunnel in the Damascus," he said.

"The Iranians are wasting time. They want their contact line to be open in Syria to send arms aid to Hamas and Hezbollah," his colleague said.

"If Iranians don't make a shit, we're going to end up in Syria in 3 or 6 months. After cutting Hezbollah we will head Lebanon and Iraq." Penter Said.

The plane was getting ready to land in Istanbul. General Izgled a high-ranking Turk intelligence officer was waiting for them in the airport. Penter got pissed off because he was waiting for Uzgol, a female intelligence agent who had affairs with Penter during previous meetings.

Penter and the Turk woman many times had left the hotel lobby to a room after official meetings. Penter had some nice memories with her. He wasn't usually very kind to women. He always expected something more than a professional negotiation from women. He even proposed to some high-ranking officials who had negative reactions.

"They've sent a male to welcome us." Penter said to his Qatarian partner while descending the plane.

Unofficial and friendly welcome ceremony was held after leaving the airstair. They immediately got on a Limousine to be transferred to a secret house in suburbs of Istanbul.

"There was a serious fight between the Free Syrian Army and a group called al-Nusra the other night," the Turk officer said on the way.

"Goddamns! Hasn't they still get to know each other?" Penter said.

"The numerous fighters from different groups has made it more complicated. They have no logic. They just fire," Izgled said.

"We spend a lot of money to train them," The Qatarian authority said.

"They must be taught to perform in a more ordered pattern. Internal conflicts will reduce the revolutionists' power," The Turk officer commented.

Penter and the Qatarian authority looked at each other in a meaning way and had nothing to say.

***

Sporadic struggles went on around the city of Aleppo and the Syrian army fought back strongly. Though it was a well-armed army, they couldn't overcome some scattered militants. The villages around Homs and Aleppo were captured by militants. The occupied areas were like ghost cities.

In a Christian district in Aleppo the militants after raping lots of captured women made them to appear in streets with burqa and complete Hijab. The women didn't dare to walk in the street. They mostly committed suicide or ran away from their town. They knew being seen by a militant means being raped.

When two Christian women were caught by some militants, one of them tried to escape but there was no use. The Arab fighter had held her arm and was dragging her to an unknown destination. Each militant touched a part of her body. A fight arose between the militants for abusing the woman and they were going to shoot each other. The women were plunders like money or jewelry. They finally agreed to use women in turn.

Two miserable women were brought to the militant's residence in order to be raped by fighters at night. The superior commanders had women during the day. They used a wet towel to delay their ejaculation.

A fighter from Somalia and another one from Aljazeera had arranged to go to "sexual pleasure center" at the night. They were sent blocks away to clear some areas. "I will fuck out the Christian women tonight," the one from Aljazeera said. "If they survive being with you I like to fuck them while beating them," his friend replied.

Suddenly a governmental Jeep showed up. The one from Somalia immediately started the gunfire and the two soldiers who were taken unaware fell down. The fighter smiled and looked happy of seeing their blood on the ground. There were moments of silence, suddenly some government soldiers appeared out of a ruined building and started gunshots toward the fighters. The Arab from Aljazeera immediately got hit and fell on the ground. The other one took shelter and threw a hand grenade toward the soldiers and killed some of them.

He was making the second grenade ready to throw when it fell off the ground from his hand. After some seconds a massive explosion throw parts of his body all around and nothing left from him.

After getting dark every coming or going in Homs and Aleppo meant nothing but death. Many houses in these districts had become the rebels' nest. They invaded the houses like attacking locusts. The houses of runaway capitalists would immediately be confiscated. Jihadis treated as hungry locusts. In a house some militants were searching the wardrobes. "Bastards! They have taken everything with them." One of them said. He shot toward each wardrobe after finding it empty.

The refrigerator was full of half empty alcoholic drinks. A fanatic fighter started shooting them when he saw non-Islamic drinks in the refrigerator. Harsh smell of alcohol filled the room. An Arab got angry and said: "You idiot, there is the smell of Najasat all over the place."

The Muslim fighters were so dull and stupid who treated worse than a drunk. A solution which one of them suggested to get rid of the smell of alcohol was to blow up the house. He placed some high explosive material inside the refrigerator and they quickly left the house. In some seconds the house exploded and the Nijasat was cleared along with the fire.

The fighters of al-Nusra like wanderer ghosts paraded aimlessly in Homs and Aleppo. The Syrian army still was present in some parts of the city. The Free Syrian army were also going city to city as revolutionist forces and sometimes their presence interfered the presence of the forces from al-Nusra which was really ridiculous.

In that desultory situation in Syria every group was fighting for his own benefits. Assad was so powerless who missed the cities of Syria one after another. He was like a drunken gambler who had missed everything but still risks for nothing.

Jolani was unsatisfied with this desultory situation. He informed Abu Ayyash the Penter's assistant via an instant message that if he encounters the forces of Abu Bakr, he would not be merciful with their lives. He also knew the runaways of Assad's army as troublemakers.

Abu Ayyash told Penter about the subject. Penter got so angry and told him to send him a message. "We all have a common purpose and that is finishing Assad's business. After that it is in our own control to determine everyone's share."

***

Abu Bakr had completely established his legal and religious government in Ar-Raqqah. But it wasn't sufficient for him. Horrible rules and religious regulations were assigned and printed as declarations, installed on walls in the main squares of the city and distributed between people. In this declaration they had asked people to observe the Islamic rules. The girls and women had to have complete Hijab. If any one of them was taken by a fighter for pleasure they didn't have the right to object. It was improper for men to shave. Having hair or bread models was announced against Sharia. It was insisted at the end of the declaration that the government doesn't want to be rigor on people but there are fields which get them closer to the heaven.

Abu Bakr's Media Communication Center named Andalus had the duty of recruitment of new jihadists from around the world. Abu Bakr ordered the Islamic propaganda association to start the recruitment. He called the head of this organization. "Let me be frank," Abu Bakr told him, "There are countless fools who are fond of bloodshed. Drag here these crazy people from around the world."

"Promise the paradise to the more wise people to seduce them," he added, "the people of the world are hungry. The pleasures don't satisfy them anymore. In

Europe and in America people are fed up and bored by sexual pleasures and they are looking for a way to repentance. Drag them all to here. Remember to pretend to be a revolutionist."

5

The youngster battalion

There was a religious training school held by an old mullah in Herat, Afghanistan to teach Quran to some children. The kids were innocent and would believe whatever sheikh told them. This school was managed by Taliban extremists.

The children were mostly orphans or one of their parents had been killed or kidnapped by Taliban. Some other parents had sent their children to this school because they had faith in such education. The education wasn't anything more than Quran. The school was situated in a ruined village with no signs of civilization. The kids brought water from well, there wasn't a bath and they had a complete primitive life.

The old sheikh as the trainer of the children talked for them about Jihad and martyrdom and mentioned that the final reward of these actions is living an eternal life in heaven. "In heaven There is only green trees, toys, milk and chocolate," he promised children, "do you like going there?"

"Yes, we love it!" Kids answered all together.

-"Good. Do you know the way?"

-"Yes, Jihad and martyrdom."

An armed young Afghan brought the phone to the sheikh. It was Abu Bakr from Ar-Raqqah who wanted to talk to sheikh. Sheikh knew him very well. Abu Bakr was with him in Afghanistan for a long time before he was called to Iraq by Zarqawi. "You are in the middle of our lesson. What is going on?" sheikh told him. "I need some fighter kids for suicide bombings. We must advance toward Homs and Aleppo and we are going to use the Iraqi method, suicide attacks," Abu Bakr said.

"You have tens of suicide women and children in Iraq. Call them," sheikh said.

"My Iraqi kids are now wandering in paradise. Without them Iraq would have been under kufr by now," Abu Bakr said.

Sheikh continued to bring excuses. "Their sending costs a lot. Iran is insecure for us. If we are caught we would be in real trouble. I don't know a secure path. If you have a way, tell me to send you some kids," he said.

"I will send an airplane and arrange everything," Abu Bakr replied.

Abu Bakr immediately called Abu Hajar and asked him to survey how they can send an airplane to Afghanistan.

"I know the way. I will tell you within an hour," Abu Hajar said.

During the next minutes Abu Hajar made a contact to Abu ayyash, Penter's assistant in Saudi Arabia and told him the story. Penter accepted every demand to struggle with Assad. Finally he accepted and they managed an airplane to transfer the children within a week.

***

The jihad fever had spread in most Arab countries. A
publicity group in Ar-Raqqah named Andalus was
trying to attract fighters from other countries. There
were hot jihadist posts on facebook and twitter to
arouse the sense of adventure between the young. In
most status and tweets they used encouraging
expressions talking about uprising against injustice to
bring despicable people to battle fields.

The wound of Syria was like an infection which had
abstracted all germs. Anyone around the world
thinking of jihad, martyrdom or Islam fled to Syria.

Gradually the Friday protests diminished and the
protestors had returned to their routine life. But
suddenly the armed groups appeared. The religious
institutions started action and backed up a bloody war
by issuing fatwas.

Gradually more and more of the young people were
deceived and turned toward jihad. Abu Bakr assigned
specific agents in Turkey to help jihadi volunteers
from other countries to pass the border and join the

training camps to be prepared by professional instructors for later wars.

It was very ridiculous. The young Arabs rushed to shamble of Syria like if they had nothing to do with their lives. The young who had grown up hardly in Arab world reached the borders of Turkey by every mean to satisfy their sense of adventure.

It was how the first phase of recruitment completed and so the fighters from Tunisia, Egypt, Palestine, Aljazeera, Morocco, Afghanistan and etc went to Syria to fight for jihadist groups like al-Nusra, Abu Bakr and the Free Syrian Army.

In this anarchy even the Syrian protestors didn't know where they were standing and no one knew who had equipped them with arms. The public opinion thought something similar to Libya would occur and these armed revolutionists would finish the job.

The authorities in Damascus were distressed. They suddenly had confronted thousands of Arab fighters in Syria like an invisible cosmopolitan army. The Arab authorities and their Turk neighbor didn't like Assad's government and counted the seconds for its fall in a way similar to the fall of Qaddafi. The estimations showed if everything went on in this way, Damascus will fall in some months. The only way out of this situation for Syria government was to ask help from their non-Arab neighbor, Iran who openly tried to protect Assad's regime.

Iran had another belief about the Arab Spring which was spreading toward Syria. Tehran Believed the case of Syria is a conspiracy. They considered the situation very well. Their intangible and invisible presence in Syria was their method. Unlike the Arab fighters who were of every category, the ordinary young Iranians didn't want to go to fronts in Syria and fight for Assad. The government of Iran also didn't expect so. In Iran Young boys and girls would prefer to spend high amounts of money on cosmetics surgeries just for self-indulgence. So they didn't care at all about politics and war in Middle East. The Tehran authorities were aware of this so they sent some professional forces to Syria to support Assad.

Gradually, by the support of Tehran being revealed, identification and targeting the Iranians inside Syria became a part of the armed fighters' program. But the Iranians weren't easy to find. A secret report by the intelligence service of an Arab country showed that Iran has sent its most skilled secret agents to Syria to plan war strategies against the Assad's opponents. Tehran had forbidden any touristic travels to Syria for its citizens for security issues. Short after the start of the crisis in Syria the beaches of this country attracted lots of young Iranians.

Al-Qaeda was one side in the quarrel in Syria which always showed up whenever there was a commotion in Arab countries. The fact is that extremism had always been spreading under the skin of Arab cities like a cancer without any outer sign. Unemployment and the consequence cultural poverty from one side and despotism from the other side had made the background of this tragic situation.

6

The immediate departure to paradise

In a desert area on the border of Iraq and Turkey there was a military training camp held by Abu Bakr and the Free Syrian Army. The volunteers would be sent to this district by buses as soon as they arrived in Turkey. These persons were regarded as bullheaded ones who were ready to take every foolish action to be sent immediately to heaven.

The camps of Abu Bakr were filled with fresh forces. The disgusting odor of body dirt and feet sweat had made an unbearable situation. The volunteers waited for being grouped and trained in a non ventilated room. They prayed, ate and slept in the same place for a while.

There were two essential courses for them: Sharia and combat.

In Sharia classes a young mufti from the Muslim brotherhood organization brain washed the persons and he was attentive for the motivations of the fighters not to be weakened.

Mufti brought quotations about jihad and martyrdom and insisted that everyone who fights and be killed for Allah, has the same dignity as ha had fought by the side of the Islam prophet.

"Now we are back to 1400 years ago," Mufti said, "our weapons are the same swords of Muhammad and his companions. Here killing every kafir is equal to getting one hundred steps closer to heaven."

"Isn't it a sin to kill the Muslims?" one of them asked.

"These people whom you are going to kill are shallow Muslims and they are indeed kafirs. They worship the dead men and shrines. The more you kill them, the more beautiful women you will have in your palace in paradise," mufti said.

By mentioning a place filled with woman most of the men were almost losing their control.

"So when does this operation start? I want to go to heaven sooner. I want to get killed to be surrounded by beautiful women in heaven and each of them asks to make love with me," an Arab from Aljazeera said.

"The start time of the operation is determined by your commanders," the mufti said.

After the Sharia class, it was the military and war training. The most terrible coarse for the new comers was to learn to behead hens in order to get ready to behead kafirs. During the day They had to have their lunch by the side of the beheaded bodies of hens. They should touch the blood and the heads.

"O.k. That's it. Beheading the kafirs is as easy as this. You must take the heads in your hands after every decapitation. You can also bring out their brains for fun," one day the commander told them.

***

There was a big map of the three countries, Syria, Iraq and Turkey on a desk in Penter's office in Saudi Arabia and as usual the Qatarian authority was beside him. They came to Riyadh after the coordination meeting in Istanbul to survey the latest developments of the Arab revolution in Syria and the results of Istanbul meeting. "We have told Jolani to be united with Abu Bakr. They don't believe that they are in a place that several other opponent groups are also there," Penter said.

"The only important thing at the moment is that the cities fall one after another which makes Assad weaker," the Qatarian authority said.

"I have a concern and that is the interference of the Iranians," Penter said.

He hopelessly laid on a sofa. "I have a repeating nightmare for several nights. We are behind the gates of Damascus and we are just some steps away from occupying Assad's palace. But suddenly the page turns and an invisible hand makes a terrible hellfire for the fighters," he said.

"You go to sleep with disturbed thoughts. It shows that going to bed without women brings you anxiety," the Qatarian authority joked.

Penter stood up. "No, we can't ignore them. We must organize the terror squads to target them," he said thoughtfully.

"The Iranians leverage their influence. We know it," the Qatarian authority said.

"I have confident information that someone named Kassim who had assisted Assad in suppressing the protests, now is in charge of the security in Damascus." Penter added.

"What can he do in front of an overflow of the fighters," The Qatarian authority said while sneering, "No, I don't think that he is this much powerful."

"We should not be surprised. We are in a hidden war with the Iranians in Lebanon," Penter continued, "They don't set aside, God damn them."

"We must isolate them," the Qatarian authority said, tired of this argument.

Penter came nearer to his companion's ear. "Keep it as a secret. We allowed the Israelis to use our air if they want to attack Iran. But those cowards haven't done anything yet. Otherwise Iran would have been completely isolated by now."

"We must arrange our propaganda somehow that a part of the Iranian opposition joins jihadis," the Qatarian authority said.

"If we can deceive the Iranian opposition and they join the fighters, it is also good for their own future, when it comes to start action for changing their own government," the Saudi authority insisted, "There is only one problem. The Iranian opposition doesn't have much Islamic tendencies."

"It seems we can't count on them," the other one said.

***

In Mecca after the Salat Dhuhr (midday prayer) in Masjid al-Haram, a Wahhabi mufti had gathered some men around him and he was talking about the value of Jihad in Syria. "Today it is clear that after the time of the prophet of Islam nothing is more precious than presence in the front in Syria. For whom is the paradise built other than jihadis and the fighters for God?" he was telling them.

"Is it obligatory to go to this jihad for me? I have a family. Who is going to feed my wife and children and supply their lives?" An Arab prayer asked.

Mufti reminded him of one of the wars at the time of the prophet. "It was the excuse of the cowards at that time. Do you want to act against the will of the God's prophet?" he said.

The Arab man started thinking. Mufti brought him and the other ones to a room some meters away from Masjid al-Haram. A young man with Arabic clothes had sat there who registered people for dispatch to Syria fronts. There was a writing on the wall behind him, "Haste to jihad."

Two Arab men, who were merchants in Mecca, after registration while leaving the mosque were cursing the Iranians and Bashar Assad. "When the Iranian pilgrims come to my shop I frown and I sell them the defected stuff," one of them said.

"I don't know why they even let the kafirs in here." His comrade said.

***

In the evening of a rather hot spring day a cargo plane which belonged to a Saudi airline landed in a far desert point in Afghanistan. Tens of suicide children were set in a queue a little far away. They all had innocent looks. They were supposed to go to Ar-Raqqah in Syria to join Abu Bakr's group.

The leader of the group named "the youngster battalion" was a militant wearing a turban who wouldn't stop putting his nonsense in the head of those children till the last moment. "Don't forget, after the suicide attack, you would see beautiful angels around you who come to you. They would put you on their wings with a kind smile and would carry you straightly to heaven."

"Is there enough things to eat and toys in heaven?" A child rose his hand and asked.

"You will be served big dishes of fruit and chocolate when you lay under the tree shadows and a river passes by your side. The taste of things are thousand times more delicious than in this world. No more question?" he asked.

The children were silent and they had no questions. They brought toward the cargo plane. The entrance was like an old abandoned depot where huge boxes were set.

The kids seemed a little anxious, apparently it was their first time to get on a plane. "Are we going to explode with the same plane?" one of them asked naively his friend.

"I think we are going to a far place to explode ourselves," one of the kids said.

When the airplane door was closed, there was complete darkness in the cabin. A sound could be heard from the place where was filled with cargos. "I think mice are celebrating our presence," a kid said.

"Remember my friends, we are going to a jihad which ends in heaven for the sake of God. So we shouldn't be afraid of anything," one of them said like he was preaching the others.

***

In Ar-Raqqah a skilled military team of 30 fighters was sent to Aleppo for reconnaissance operation. They reached a ruined village on their way which was controlled by another Islamic group. Abu Bakr's men who had worn local clothes and had covered their faces, passed that point by introducing themselves as native revolutionists.

Some kilometers away, two tanks with a flag of the Syrian government was moving forward. The fighters decided to make a trap for them. The tanks were getting closer accompanied by two military jeeps. The fighters prepared some side road bombs to place on the way of the tanks. Then they moved back to a place where they could quickly start shooting after the explosion of the bombs. The tanks proceeded slowly and poor soldiers didn't know that they would be killed in some minutes.

The tanks got forward and in a second the light of an explosion lightened the dark of the night. The unremitting gunfire of fighters toward the soldiers started. The governmental soldiers immediately sheltered behind a small hill. The tanks were burning in fire and no one knew if the ones inside them had been killed or had escaped.

Some violent militants quietly rounded the hill where the soldiers had sheltered. The soldiers were shooting forward and they wasn't cautious to their back. After some seconds their gunfire stopped. They were trapped but not killed at the moment.

"We'll have a blood feast," a fighter said.

"If you are a Syrian compatriot, please have merci on me," a soldier who was extremely frightened was begging a fighter.

The masked fighter was laughing. it was evident there was no merci.

He throw his gun aside and brought a dirk out. A major and a servant were also captured.

"Chenchal" a Pakistani violent fighter who was the ex-leader of a group who was responsible for the massacre of Shiites, suggested to have a big blood feast. His comrades started shooting in the air in order to show their agreement.

He put the dirk under the first victim's neck. "Dear God accept this sacrifice from me and reward me beautiful angels in heaven in return," he said.

In some seconds there was a sea of blood. The decapitated head fell on the ground and the fighters spit on it.

Now it was the turn of two other captives who had been held on their knees with blindfolded eyes and tightened hands waiting for their death.

This time another fighter from Chechen, brought out a big sickle. He ran to the captive sergeant and beheaded him in a moment. The decapitated head fell on the ground while still the pupil was moving. A fighter tossed it and controlled it on his foot like he was playing football.

The fighters were dancing with their swords. Now it was the third captive's turn. An Arab fighter from Morocco said that this time he wants to use a DShK as the tool for beheading. He started the gunshot and the head was hanging on the body afterwards. The decapitated heads were put in front of the vehicles. It was a shocking scene. The heads were staring up with eyes wide open.

***

In an insecure path 35 kilometers far from Damascus, a bus carrying some Iranians was stopped by jihadis. The attackers were so dumb that they couldn't distinguish the nationality of the passengers. "Which way do you go?" A fighter who had covered his face asked while he was inspecting the bus.

"We are electrical engineers," replied a passenger with a heavy Arabic accent, "we are going near Damascus to install and test some utility pole and power lines."

The fighter was convinced and let them pass after checking their documents.

Only a few moments after the bus passed, a message was sent to the inspection station commander. They were told that a bus containing some Iranian security agents are supposed to pass that district. It was insisted that they speak fluent Arabic and they carry fake Syrian documents.

The one who received the message dropped the walkie-talkie and ran to the Arab soldier who had let them pass. "Damn you! Didn't you really understand those passengers were Iranians?" he shouted.

"It's impossible. They spoke Arabic better than Syrians." The young fighter replied.

"You'll be hanged if they won't get caught by tomorrow," the commander threatened him.

Some Toyota pickups moved quickly. A group of them took a bypath and they could finally stop the bus.

They made the Iranians to get out of the bus violently and lay them on the ground. An Arab started tying their hands rapidly. He kept swearing Iranians with his Arab accent.

All the identification papers were checked. An ID with a weapon logo was found between the papers of one of them. "Are you in a military mission?" a rough fighter asked.

"We are electrical engineers, we are going to install utility poles," the Iranian answered.

The fighter put a dreadful pistol on his head. "Mean liar!" he said.

The fighters commander was waiting for the arrested Iranians in the base. "Isn't there a woman among you?" he asked one of the captives as soon as they arrived.

"Our women don't come to such places," an Iranian answered.

The rough commander kicked him in the face with his military boots. The blood covered his face.

They decide to make a movie about the Iranians being captive by the military and send it to TV channels.

***

7

Cancer under the skin

In Ar-Raqqah Abu Bakr had lounged on a sofa in a seized fancy house and was looking at a book and noted something time to time. Abu Hajar knocked the door and entered. As usual he wanted to know if Abu Bakr needs anything or not.

"I see you are hardly working on the Islamic State Manifesto," Abu Hajar said.

Abu Bakr put the book aside. "Yes, I was reading some pages about the manner of the prophet of Islam and his companions. These are lessons we must apply them practically in our government over the world in order to show the real ace of Islam."

Abu Hajar, who couldn't understand these things by his tiny sense and understanding, took a wise gesture. "The governments nowadays are shameful. Now it is really time to plan to destroy them all. Why earthquakes or devastating storms never happen in Europe or other western countries?" he asked Abu Bakr.

Abu Bakr got angry. "What was the Hurricane Katrina then? I bet it wasn't a hurricane. The cries of the Satan destroyed them all. Look at Iran. It is the land of Kafirs. Don't you see the earthquakes? the draught? They pray to have a drop of rain. Are you blind or you pretend to see nothing?" Abu Bakr said.

Abu Hahjar was playing with louses inside his long beard. He was just going to understand what Abu Bakr meant. "Yes, also destructive floods in Europe. I think God isn't patient in front of the Kafirs," he admitted.

"The god has given his sword in our hands. He doesn't enter the war in person. We are his sword to decapitate kafirs," Abu Bakr said.

"I'm sure when we establish our Islamic caliphate, coward kafirs will join us in groups. We will decapitate the rebellious ones and recruit the good ones," Abu Hajar said.

"Everyone will obey us," Abu Bakr added.

Abu Bakr asked about the latest news from the war fronts. "Tens of kilometers of the way from Ar-Raqqah toward Aleppo has been cleared. We will advance with no problem," Abu Hajar explained."

He also asked about the suicide kids and if their training had been started and if they are being prepared for suicide attacks.

"Hit them, if they weren't listening. These mulish kids will live just some days more. Don't care for them," Abu Bakr said.

"Don't worry. They are obedient and they imagine paradise in their dreams. They have been so brainwashed that they are impatient to get killed," Abu Hajar said.

***

In a point between Aleppo and Homs, the forces from al-Nusra and the Free Syrian Army confronted each other. It was ridiculous. The high-ranked commanders of the two groups were supposed to have a meeting in a village house. The representatives of the Free Syrian Army were men with military uniforms, shaved faces and thick moustaches. On the other hand the representatives of al-Nusra seemed like the ones who had just came out of bed. They attended at the negotiation table with dirty beards and masked faces.

"Rahman" an officer from the Free Syrian Army asked the fighters to remove their mask. "Abu Kasif" whose long beard could be seen under the fabric mask, ignored Rahman. "We are ready to listen to you," he said.

"Apparently you are moving like our shadows where ever we go," General said.

"We have been in Syria for years. Where did you show up from?" Kasif said.

The general was confused. "We all have a common goal and a common enemy. We must not fight each other," he said, "What is your suggestion?"

"Set aside where ever we arrived and let us go forward," Kasif said.

The two groups agreed not to stand in the way of each other. The commander of al-Nusra forces didn't guarantee that his men wouldn't shoot any of them by mistake. "Everything is possible. Inaccurate shooting, unexpected fights because of not recognizing each other," he said.

"Exactly like what we did to you before," the general said.

"If you even think of it one more time, I'll behead you all before any other action," Kasif said.

The al-Nusra commander reported the results of the meeting to Jolani. "My most inquietude is about al-Baghdadi forces who are sticking to us," Jolani, the al-Nusra leader said.

"If you order to massacre them, I won't let anyone of them," Kasif said.

"Wait now," Jolani added.

The leader of al-Nusra put a message in the draft box of the e-mail for al-Zawahiri in an opportunity. Putting the messages in the draft and not sending them was to prevent the intelligence services of the United States to track the content of their messages.

"We are still faithful to the path of the great martyr of Islam Bin Laden," Jolani wrote in his message, "But this villain rat, al-Baghdadi, dreams of the leadership of al-Qaeda. He doesn't obey you and he is wandering like stray rats in Syria and makes troubles for Jihadts."

Ayman al-Zawahiri the leader of al-Qaeda ordered Jolani to avoid any battle with Abu Bakr al-Baghdadi. "Leave him alone," He wrote in a draft mail, "I called this unwise person from Iraq to Syria in order to ease the fall of Assad. If you start quarreling, the other secular armed groups would win the fight with Assad and that is not what we want."

Jolani was the docile good boy of al-Zawahiri who had no choice other than admitting his boss instructions. He had two important parts of Aleppo under control. His group ruled upon Sharia in every part they captured. Their extremism had made the life of the people in captured areas like hell.

There were no sign of life in the cities which had came out of the government control. There was no water, no power. The stores were plundered. The banks and financial centers were closed. People ran away from each city where the fighters got close to. Because if the city fell they would have been captured by fighters who knew nothing of the civilization.

The most merciless and fool persons, had held the Islam flag under the name of jihadist groups and they killed all the opponents with the most tiny excuse.

Al-Nusra under the leadership of Jolani was in fact the branch of al-Qaeda in Syria which was present in this country long before the commotions. And the ridiculous point was that, Assad was aware of their presence but he did nothing about it.

After the start of the protests in Syria, Jolani got the mission by Ayman al-Zawahiri to occupy Damascus and establish a government like Taliban in Syria. The branch of al-Qaeda in Iraq, Abu Bakr al-Baghdadi also got the mission to make this country insecure by spreading terrorism and suicide attacks after the exit of the Americans. Al-Zawahiri who had replaced Bin Laden Asked Iraq and Syria to coordinate each other. After the death of Bin Laden, al-Qaeda activated scattered networks of terrorists in Afghanistan, Pakistan, Iraq, Syria, Saudi Arabia, Yemen and around Russia. After the chaos in Arabic countries, the terrorists from al-Qaeda came out like cockroaches .

There was a mess in Syria. Everyone organized a rebel group with ten armed men. Al-Nusra got some other small groups under its control, one of them was the Khorasani fighters. The members of this group after September 11th attacks went secretly to Iran. But the government of Iran soon noticed their presence in Iran and kept them under house arrest.

The extremist Islamists were a hidden danger in the middle east which became apparent after the crisis in Syria like an Abscess which finally shows up after an internal infection. Hundreds of fighter groups were active in the middle east with different thoughts and beliefs. Disillusioned young Arabs specially from the north of Africa were deceived by seductive mottos of the jihadist groups. Most of them were just eager to enter the paradise as soon as possible. They were told that if they get killed in jihad they would immediately enter the heaven and plenty of women would wait there for them.

***

Abu Bakr and his men captured Ar-Raqqah planning to proceed to other points. The fighters were trained before. He had ordered a volunteer aware of the Salafi rulings to express subjects about jihad, martyrdom and heaven for fighters in order to motivate them. The brain washing of the forces started. The fighters were told that they can feel the smell of heaven from here and beautiful girls are awaiting their entrance.

Abu Bakr assigned a governor for Ar-Raqqah and went forward with thousand of forces. His men moved toward the districts occupied by other rebels. They passed by a region occupied by the Free Syrian Army. The Commander of the army under the control of Abu Bakr sent messengers to the inspection stations of the Free Syrian Army. The message was that they all were fighting to realize the goals of the people of Syria. After hours of progress they reached an almost empty village with no conflict. They were supposed to stay there waiting for a group of fresh forces.

There wasn't any habitable place in the village. So some tents were held to accommodate the fighters. The village seemed abandoned and all the inhabitants were killed or escaped. The tramp dogs were looking for food or a rotten bone of human among the ruins. Abu Bakr were lying in his tent on a big pillow and continued reading his book. He was reading a book about the manner of prophet in wars and trying to simulate his method by his.

Jolani was very angry of the reports about the progress of Abu Bakr army toward Aleppo.

His forces had some parts of Aleppo under their control. The reconnaissance teams of al-Nusra had informed Jolani that Abu Bakr forces are proceeding toward Aleppo. Abu Bakr was planning a pincer movement to completely dominate Aleppo though he didn't want to confront Jolani. His plan was to ignore the annoying groups on his way who were fighting with Assad and just pass by their side without any conflict. He was waiting for fresh jihadis to easily perform his plans.

***

The recruitment of jihadi fighters from Arab world to join the fighters was something normal in Syria.

In the border area of Turkey and Syria, there was a bus terminus where disordered bus services were available for the new fighters. The representatives of different jihadist groups were present in this point and were holding banners to attract the adrift fighters to join their groups.

"Islam's jihadists" was written on one of these banners.

They were like tour leaders holding their banners to attract the fighters toward their buses. There were also leaders waiting for jihadis from other groups, al-Nusra, Ahrar, Free Syrian Army, The prophet's Guardians and etc.

Sometimes the leaders quarreled to reach fighters. They ended up threatening each other in a stupid way. Daily ten to fifteen fighters joined jihadist groups.

Bashar Assad the leader of Syria, had a weak army. The army missed every day the control of a part of the country. There was a rumor around the country that the family of the president had left the country.

In these days a skilled military-intelligence agents from Iran easily entered Damascus. They went directly to the presidential palace from the airport. The Iranians didn't pass any of the security gates in the airport. The guard soldiers saluted them. There was a mysterious face among them. It has been told that he was always in charge of exterritorial missions.

The four men directly entered the president's office and Bashar embraced them. The president was calm and there was no signs of anxiety on his ace. "We are suddenly attacked by rats. Our security and peace have disappeared and I prefer to consult close friends." he said.

"By your permission, the situation is now completely under our control," the high-ranked Iranian named Kassim said.

He brought a map of Syria out of his bag and installed it on the wall. On the map the captured areas were shown in red.

"Seemingly the situation is really bad," Bashar said wondered, "What does the army do then?"

"There has been an insidious coalition against you which is now under control," Kassim said.

"The rats play inside the circle. There is nothing to worry in your united government," another Iranian general said.

"We were informed that Abu Bakr is planning to attack Aleppo. Al-Nusra and Free Syrian Army has occupied parts of Aleppo and Homs," Kassim continued.

"How long does it take for them to reach here if they continue on this speed?" Bashar asked joking.

"If they don't conflict each other, they will be here soon," Kassim said.

"What do you suggest?" Bashar asked worrying.

Kassim stood up and looked at the map carefully. "At present, our priority is to keep Damascus and the contact line with resistance," Kassim said.

Bashar smiled.

"Passing each point of the lines that we have specified is a step into the hell for them," one of the two Iranians accompanying Kassim said.

"We can keep them outside the gates of Damascus for years until they finally lose their motivation," Kassim said to Bashar.

"I don't like being surrounded by dirty rats," Bashar nodded.

"They will be soon destroyed," Kassim said, "Don't worry."

8

Marriage in stable

There was a real chaos in Abu Bakr al-Baghdadi's camp. His forces had gathered from all nations and they could understand each other. In one of these nights in a village at war, some fighters had been stricken by sensual thoughts. They contacted a mufti in Tunisia via Skype.

Mufti was wearing a loose dress and had a disgusting look in his eye. "We are in Syria for Jihad." a fighter told him

"Good for you!" Answered mufti, "God will reward you. If you get killed, you'll accompany the prophet men in paradise."

"We are in extreme need of sex, but there isn't any woman around," the fighter said.

"Isn't in all that ruin a girl or even an old woman for you?" sheikh asked.

The fighter replied: "Nothing but wandering ghosts and some stables."

"We're gonna fuck ourselves." a fighter from the north of Africa added.

"Wait for some seconds," Mufti said then he turned pages of a book like he was looking for an order or Islamic ruling. "You are in a compulsion and war condition, there are rules for these situations in Islam. .Satisfy your needs with livestock preferably cows or horses!" After some seconds he said

Then he repeated a phrase in Arabic multiple times and asked them to say it before intercourse.

The three fighters rushed to stable to fuck the miserable animals. The shouts of animals went to the sky. When a fighter was getting close to a horse from behind he was kicked badly to the ground by horse but his sexual desire made him stood up again and try his chance one more time. Finally the men returned at their place tired and sexually satisfied and fell into a deep sleep.

There was a total disaster. Abu Bakr didn't find it reasonable to stay in a loose village around Aleppo. Finally he commanded for attack in a relatively hot afternoon. The suicide children got on the tanks. Vehicles and Toyota pickups armed with machine guns started moving. Some Kilometers away the conflicts started. The governmental forces prevent their advance. The battle got worse and continued for hours causing casualties from both sides. Finally the governmental forces setback and Abu Bakr men advanced kilometers inside the city

His commands were announced directly by Abu Hajar and he never appeared personally in front of his army, thus his men only had heard his name.

After getting dark a massive storm with a lot of dust surrounded the city. The fighters started to search the houses. Some of the tribes who wasn't pleased of the government stayed in the town and accompanied the rebels.

Always in this situation there are unsatisfied groups in a country who help the enemies unwarily without knowing the subsequences of their acts. Some tribes went to Abu Bakr to take the oath of allegiance. The occupied homes in town became the fighters' residence. They had holes in walls of the houses and installed the gun cameras inside them to shoot any suspicious points.

The beds of ex-citizens had became the lounge for fighters. They did nasty things to the ladies wear. In an occupied house one of them took a piece of clothes with his barrel. "I want the owner of this," he said. Then he started rubbing the clothes on his belly.

"I hope to have dozens of them in paradise," another fighter said.

"Now we have nothing but livestock, What the hell I will do if I find a woman in this city."

A little while before the dawn adhan, Abu Bakr woke up to read some pages of Islam history and review his previous notes. Once in a while an explosion or gunfire could be heard. His assistant Abu Hajar also couldn't sleep. He was in a continuous contact with war commanders.

Abu Hajar entered Abu Bakr's room. "The tracers which have been attached to the fighters' arms show that they have mistaken the battlefield with marital bed," he said.

Abu Bakr let the book aside. "What is going on then?" he asked.

- The fighters has invaded the cows and horses in the village where we stayed before.

- A serious decision must be taken. I had allowed them to have every woman as a war plunder. The women have distracted the fighters' attention, they must be released of this sexual need to focus on war.

"I think a fatwa can solve the problem." Abu Hajar suggested.

"Fatwa solves the problem when the tool is available. Most of girls and women have escaped the war zone, they must have had an order from somewhere." Abu Bakr replied.

***

In Aleppo the advance of Abu Bakr's group had encountered obstacles. They thought of Iraqi-Pakistani method to move forward, which meant to use suicide attacks. For this mean, the suicide children from youngster battalion were easily available. 20 Afghani children plus 7 orphans whom they had found from all over Syria were good options for suicide attacks.

Abu Bakr ordered the children to put on explosive belts and pretend to be poor and homeless children who wander in ruins, looking for a piece of bread or playing with other children. Then they had to get close to governmental centers and explode them.

The children were told that an angel from paradise has came to take them. Thus they must not delay the angel and they should be rapid and join the angel sooner to reach the paradise.

Some children set their next meeting in paradise for playing. "I will ask the angel to take me to the field where is full of grapes." One of them said to his friend.

Another one said: "I like to go there sooner to meet my parents once again. My dad went to paradise after a mission and my mum disappeared too. But I know that they are waiting for me in paradise."

Their enthusiasm to wear the vests were astonishing. They even pushed each other to be the first one to do the job. The reconnaissance team had specified the important point as many as the children. With these explosions they could move forward, also tens of governmental soldiers would be killed.

The most important places were some entrance passages in Aleppo named "Bab al-Salam" and "Tal Abyad". These regions had been held by government forces or other jihadist groups time to time. Assad's men had moved the front line kilometers away from Damascus to prevent any danger to capital. As soon as the number of casualties had been increased they would retreat and let the opponents to have more land.

It was around a hot noon when the children with their unkempt appearance were sent to the determined points. Everything seemed regular. The soldiers stared at every moving point frightened and even a bird or a cat would make them suspect. The only thing they wouldn't suspect was some innocent children who were getting close to them.

The soldiers thought they were homeless orphans without any family due to war. The children seemed cool. They moved to the supposed place while playing with a ball. When they got so close to outpost, a soldier notified them to play further. The children were educated and they knew what to do exactly. One of them threw the ball inside the area under the control of soldiers and ran immediately into the enclosure. Then instead of picking the ball he hit himself to a trench wall. There was a massive explosion. After some seconds his play mate did the same to a group of soldiers who were trying to find a shelter after seeing that scene.

The soldiers fell on the ground one after another and nothing was left from the children bodies. An operation group of Abu Bakr's fighters were ready to interfere and take the passage under control. They shot the remaining soldiers. And it was so that some strategic points of Aleppo became under the control of the fighters.

After the mission Abu Hajar went to Abu Bakr and declared: "The children now went to heaven with angels and we dominated some strategic points."

"Clear everything in kilometers away." Abu Bakr replied, "Behead every soldier who come in your view."

Then Abu Hajar added a shocking news: "The fighters who had sexual intercourse with animals, are suffering serious diseases. Their whole body is covered with black dots and they are in severe pain."

Abu Bakr swore them and ordered to burn them quietly. "They probably had chosen the ill animals." He said. "The idiots, if they had waited, the women would have arrived."

9

Sexual jihad fatwa

In a religious student training center in Tunisia which was managed by Muslim Brotherhood organization some muftis and clergymen had got together after the prayer and was reading Hadith and Quran. A gentle wind blew and shot the door which was half open.

The young clergymen were a little afraid. In this moment the power was also cut. A mufti got up to light a lantern.

"Dear brothers when the door was closed the soul of a martyr from the era of beginning of Islam entered the room. He shot the door and turn off the lights in order not to be seen," an old mufti who was the trainer of the young men said.

Suddenly all young clergymen stood up to respect the ghost. Apparently the ghost had found a place to sit among them.

"Whenever wind blows divine ghosts descend to earth to be with faithful people," the old mufti said.

There was still dark all over the place and only the dim light of the lantern lightened the room. Old mufti reported the ghosts situation in every moment: "Now the majestic soul would like to participate in our debate and give us his suggestions if necessary."

The mufti who had ordered the fighters to have relations with animals in Syria asked: "As we all know at the moment Muslim fighters are doing jihad in fronts in Syria, but they have a major problem."

"The martyr's soul is now concerned. Let us know what is our fighters' problem," the mufti who was observing the guest ghost situation said.

"They are in urgent need to satisfy their sensual demands. The lust has reduced their power for fight. They asked me for a solution and I gave them an order," the bad looking young mufti continued.

There was an strange voice like a cuckoo sound. The mufti in the role of interpreter said that was the martyr's soul crying. "And what did you suggest them?" he asked.

"I allowed intercourse with livestock" the young mufti answered, "They have just a little cooled down in stable."

At this moment a door creak was heard. No one had left the room. But it was like if someone had exited or entered. Some one thought maybe another ghost had joined them.

The big mufti immediately reported that the ghost had left, "We will wait some minutes for him to rejoin us."

The young clergymen were whispering between each other when the ghost's return was delayed. Then the mufti announced: "The martyr's soul had an urgent call so he had to return to sky immediately. But he asked me to solve the fighters' problem as soon as possible. Are there any suggestions?"

"I think according to situation we can make masturbation lawful," One of muftis said.

"That's the easiest way." the old mufti said. "It's like telling a hungry man to eat bread with water."

The other mufti who had ordered intercourse with animals insisted: "My suggestion is still the livestock. It is an emergent order during the war."

"It is like telling a hungry man to eat hay," The old mufti said.

No one had a new suggestion. They thought the best way is to be patient until the fall of Assad, when they can use women as sex slaves. "Enough! Leave your foolish suggestions and listen to my idea." the old mufti who had became tired yelled.

They all got quiet to know what his solution was. He hesitated a little and drank some water. "I order the Jihad al-Nikah." He continued, "Now it is obligatory for all Muslims to send their wives and daughters to Syria in order to satisfy the sexual needs of fighters. Everyone does so will be in heaven, and who ever abstains will burn in hell fire forever."

A clergyman got embarrassed of this suggestion. "For the start you first send your wife and daughter to be a sample for others," he said.

The old mufti who had been surprised, called the man next to him. "You're a fool. This order is only for common people to solve this problem," he whispered in his ears.

The day after the Jihad al-Nikah law was issued, the mosques in Tunisia started the propaganda to recruit women. There was a recruitment table in front of mosques to register volunteer women.

"Ladies, If you want to end up, in heaven recruit for Jihad al-Nikah" a big banner in front of the mosque said.

The women referred to the registration desk and asked about it. A complete covered woman approached the table. "I'm married. Can I join the Jihad al-Nikah?" She asked.

The young man in charge of registration took a greedy look to woman. "You're married, your reward is twice."

"Am I going to marry a fighter?" she asked.

- "There are many fighters. You may be with multiple ones."

The woman registered. "I try to persuade my husband"

The registration guy answered shamelessly: "There is no need to persuade your husband. You are going to jihad. Run away from home if you want to go to paradise."

The same answer was given to other women too. The muftis arranged it somehow that volunteer women would be at their service before departure for Syria. Their excuse was Nikah before intercourse which seemed more an opportunistic way to abuse women. The women were told that there were seven obstacles to reach heaven. "Three of them are passed by this Nikah, Three of them would be passed by Jihad al-Nikah and the one last obstacle needs your faith and prayer."

An old sheikh who was in charge of sending the group of jihadist women to Syria, had established these rules. He had told that every volunteer woman's body must be checked before being sent. He intended to impose himself on these women before sending them to Syria.

After two weeks of registration, some groups of Tunisian women were sent. The old Sheik had kept some of those girls and women by different excuses and by giving various fatwas. He had issued documents for them which guaranteed their entrance to paradise. In these certifications the name of the woman was written and the title was "The certification to enter the paradise" and the document was signed and sealed. "Do you want heaven? It is your entrance document," he told the women.

"Staying with me is as rewarding as taking part in jihad. You will directly go to heaven," Sheikh told them.

Some of the women stayed by his side with these promises and gave him the services he wanted. Sheikh ate lots of date everyday to be strong enough to have intercourse with several women. He assaulted those women shamelessly.

When the group of the women were ready they attended courses to be taught what they must do. A young religion student had received a fatwa from the great sheikh which let these students to benefit women. This fatwa was named Nikah before jihad. According this fatwa the volunteer women before Nikah with jihadis in Syria should have intercourse with muftis or young religious students in order to be ready to fully satisfy the fighters.

It was evidently prostitution but the women had believed in jihad somehow that they didn't think of it in this way.

In the classes the women were told to eat nourishing nutrients like dates and meat to be strong in bed in front of the fighters. Eating sour food and lemon was forbidden. The women had no more anxiety after their first intercourse with the students. "You may be used in Syria by several men in a group. You just must let the jihadis enjoy what they want," The sheikh told them.

One day the mufti in charge of sending women was walking across the religious school yard while putting his hand on his back. He saw a young student who was eager to go to Syria for fighting.

"Do you want to get yourself killed just for women?" mufti told him.

The young student smiled." I'm looking forward so much. Even imagining having sex with multiple women is exciting for me," he said.

"What can I do? Go to Syria to be with those women."

"Dear sheikh, give me some of these women to take them with me to Syria."

The sheikh got angry. "You and others had sex with these women and you still want more. How do you dare ask it?" he said.

The young student apologized and continued his way. Mufti was nagging. He couldn't stand straight being exhausted of relations with women.

10

The woman who buried the jihadis alive

The invading fighters were only thinking of reaching a woman. Basically they had came to Syria promised by beautiful girls and women in heaven . They were told the sooner they get killed the sooner they can reach those women in paradise.

The fighters were allowed to seize any woman they saw in the captured areas before the time they go to paradise.

"Khaledeh" was one of those women who lived alone in the suburbs of captured Aleppo. After the forces of Abu Bakr entered the city, Khaledeh knew they were waiting for opportunity to reach women. She didn't dare to exit her house even for daily buys. Nevertheless she got caught once she left her house.

As soon as the fighters noticed a girl fully covered under burqa, they invaded her. One of them tried to touch her pretending he wants to search her. Khaledeh refused. "I don't want your dirty hands to touch me," she said.

One of the fighters held her arm and was trying to touch other parts of her body. The other fighter put his gun on her head. Everyone knew that they could easily kill anyone.

One of them took a serious tone and tried to legalize their job. "Why did you came alone in the streets?" he said.

-"I have no one. My family were all killed and I live alone."

The fighters seemed satisfied. "We must search your house," they said.

An Arab immigrant with a deformed body who had covered his face with a dirty red fabric came forward. "The sentence of going outside without a man is 70 lashes. If we catch you, you'll be whipped in public," he said.

Khaledeh was going to burst in tears. "Your only way to survive is to take us to your house and to entertain us," he said shamelessly.

The four fighters accompanied the girl to her house. On the way some other fighters blocked their way to have a part of their prey. "How long does it take to do your job?" The strange fighter said, "Give her to us after you are done."

One of the four men accompanying the girl took out his gun and pointed it to the stranger. "The slave is ours," he said, "Repeat your request If you want a bullet in your head."

They continued their way. "Are you Muslims?" Khaledeh asked the men accompanying her.

"What did you think? Are we like Kafirs?" One of them replied.

"It is forbidden to get close to non-maharim in Islam. Leave me alone for god sake," Khaledeh said.

"We have the legal law for this thing and now we are permitted to have you," a fighter said with an Afghani-Arabic accent.

They arrived home. Khaledeh guided the men into the bedroom. Four nasty men had their heads in the cloud . They had taken off their military coats and were lying on bed. "I'll be there when you are ready." the woman said from outside.

"Better not to make it so long, we don't have much time," one of men said.

Some minutes passed. Dreaming of coming events had distracted the fighters so much that they didn't mention the woman's delay. They were so out of their minds that they didn't think of a guard for woman. "There may be a trick," finally one of them said.

One of them came out of the room for inspection. There was no trace of woman. He returned immediately. "The fucking chick has disappeared," told to his comrades.

The four men searched all the house like dumbs who had lost everything.

"We should have bumped her in the street and burnt her body after that," one of them said.

The half naked men were looking outside when Khaledeh appeared in the window, "Where are you then? I'm ready." she addressed the men.

The frenzied fighters rushed into the house. The door was locked. They had no choice other than shooting it open but they couldn't find her inside. They were completely out of their minds and they started shooting all around the place. "If we reach you, we will stone you for three days in the city," one of them shouted.

"After we're done with her, I will behead her by my own hands," a young Arab continued.

They went on searching and they found at the end of the house a small door leading to a tunnel which wasn't clear where it ended. "I think we have found her," one of them called the others.

"She couldn't have been hidden anywhere but here," the other one said while smiling.

They entered the tunnel one after another and looked for woman in narrow dark corridor. The air was heavy with the harsh sewage smell. They moved on without noticing getting far of the door they had entered. The more they advanced, the unbearable sewer gas would become and they practically couldn't breathe anymore. "I can't go on, I return," one of them said while panting.

Two others were coughing. The narrow dark tunnel after a long distance reached a wider corridor. Their little torch couldn't help them find the way. They finally returned the path they had came. But the way seamed close. They were panicked. The previous path was filled with soil and they couldn't return to the first point.

"She was a monster," an Arab said, "we are imprisoned like doomed."

"Don't worry," one of them told his friends who had believed it was the end of their lives, "we'll be in heaven in a short while. The beautiful heaven women will welcome us."

Inside the house Khaledeh was cleaning her kitchen and the entrance of tunnel which she had filled hardly.

11

The sick prostitutes mission

Jihad al-Nikah made so many ones angry amongst them the enemies of foreign fighters in Syria. An intelligent service organization who always followed the Jihadist fighters activities, planned something weird.

It was around 2 A.M. outside a secret house in Beirut where some elite spies from countries in middle east had got together. They were totally four and they all spoke Arabic fluently. The meeting was held in order to discuss the Jihad al-Nikah and the ways to confront it.

"We must give them a lesson, these womanizer jihadists," one of the spies said, "we are all here to wash out this Fatwa unclean "

"I have consulted some whorehouses in Qafqaz district," another spy said who had a gross body and harsh voice while he was coughing continuously, "they introduced me 80 sick women who suffer from disgusting diseases like Syphilis, Gonorrhea and etc."

"We will give these jihadi bastards some fatal diseases," another one said with a calm voice, "in the hell their stench will annoy the other hellish people."

"We may have a big problem," another one who wore thick glasses continued, "These idiots kill to go to heaven. What if they really end up in heaven? Then they would understand our nasty trick. What then?"

There was only silence in the room for some seconds. "They would mess up the heaven if they find their way there," one of them said with a grin.

The man with a gross body was really angry of the women who had volunteered for Jihad al-Nikah. "I really want these rubbish women to be punished," he said, "We must handle the events so that the fighters go to these women after their relations with sick women. So they would be also infected by diseases."

"I've heard so many women had escaped their homes to join for these sexual services," a spy said, "It's a disaster."

The suspicious men agreed on doing their best to ruin the process of Jihad al-Nikah.

***

Jolani, the leader of al-Nusra had been in a prostration for a long while and he seemed to be likely to stay in this position forever. One of his assistants suddenly entered the room. "Dear sheikh, There is a message for you from al-Zawahiri the leader of al-Qaeda." he said.

Jolani immediately got up like he was thinking about everything but God during his prostration. "Did you bring the print?" he said to his assistant with a warning look.

"No, I just wanted to inform you."

Jolani laid on the ground and grabbed his forehead to the floor. After some moments he got up and went to his laptop, opened his mail and looked for the al-Qaeda leader's message in the draft folder.

Al Zawahiri had wrote to him:

I know that you have captured some parts of Syria at the moment, but you haven't done anything for Islam yet. While it's your duty to execute the Islamic laws word by word and not to postpone them with the excuse of war. Don't compromise with people against Islam. The earth is ours in future, don't forget it and be sure that lots of nations will be under our control.

After reading the mail, Jolani recalled his senior advisors. They decided to gather all the men in charge of the captured areas. The meeting took place after some hours at night. The leader of al-Nusra addressed the five administrators of occupied districts, "I want you to execute full Islamic laws in your territories," he said.

"What do you mean?" one of them asked, "We don't have any organization for Implementation of Sharia."

"For example the young people are not allowed to wear short-sleeved shirts," Jolani continued, "Or women are not allowed to appear in the streets without burqa or without a man accompanying them. The men should not shave and they have to have beards as long as a finger length."

"We get the women who are seen alone," a district's administrator said, "Or if we find a woman with a pleasant face or body, we would kill her man to capture her."

"This is legal for you in Sharia," Jolani said, "but if you wait the sex slaves will be here in some days."

"In some offices men and women work together and they talk to each other," another one said.

"Whip them and let them know how heinous they are," Jolani said angrily, "The women have no right to work outside the house."

"I have even seen some cases of drinking wine," another one added, "they easily sell alcoholic beverages."

"The consumer and the seller must be whipped for three days when they are hanged upside down,"

Jolani said, "Cut hand and leg of the thieves, and the penalty of not going to the prayer of Jumu'ah is whipping."

"They have became careless and remiss under the Assad's governing," another one said, "They are unfamiliar with Sharia."

"Organize a committee for Enjoining good and forbidding wrong" Jolani said, "you must know what Islam has asked us, idiots."

In the next days there were big banners in the city to call people to get together in big squares. In one of these meetings in the city of Homs, a violent commander who had covered his face addressed the crowd, "Didn't you want the Islamic government?" he said, "Weren't you tired of Assad?"

Suddenly there was a rumble in the crowd. "Booh! We don't want you, go away!" everyone shouted.

The angry commander started shooting in the air. People got quiet. "Now on no one is allowed to do anything in contrary of Sharia," the man said,

"Whoever does not obey the rules would confront whipping, imprisonment and decapitation."

There was again a noise in the crowd. This time the armed fighters went between the crowd and started beating some guys. They started to execute the rules from that exact moment and the men who hadn't long beard were trapped like mice. A fighter attacked the young people who had worn short-sleeved shirts with a whip. The girls and women without a man accompanying them were dragged to an unknown place. And so the orders of Jolani were performed.

***

Abu Bakr and his men in Aleppo were counting every moment for the women of Jihad to arrive. One of them were assigned to register the fighters who wanted the women. There were tokens designed and distributed among the fighters. Each token were usable or five times of intercourse.

They also had done a skillful trickery. While the relationship of a woman with multiple men is forbidden in Islam, a fatwa from fool muftis not only had allowed it but also it commented that it could have been rewarded by paradise.

A fighter brought a print from a Wahhabi mufti in Saudi Arabia. He said upon this legal ruling he wants to have sex with five women who had sex with his comrades. His demand was recorded but he was told to keep the fatwa for himself, because there would be a real mess if everyone asked such a thing.

More than one thousand of "sex tokens" had been prepared. The person who didn't have the token, didn't have the right to have sex with any of the jihadist women.

Abu Bakr received a fatwa from his favorite mufti in Saudi Arabia who had emphasized that fighters had no right to use any pregnancy prevention tool like condoms while being with their jihadist wives.

The sheikh had ordered the women to be pregnant and give birth to children who would fight for Islam goals in future. By this rule the fighters were getting ready a warrior generation from the Nikah with the jihadist women.

***

In the evening of a rather hot day a thick dust had covered the sky. Two buses reached the border of Turkey each of thme carrying forty women. The spies had arranged everything. The women had lunch and stayed for some hours in a resort. Some of them took their medicine and a group of them had itchy parts.

A little far away the agents from rebel groups in Syria was waiting impatiently for women from Tunisia to be at the service of the jihadist fighters.

The sick prostitutes were uninvited guests who were supposed to have sex with rebels before the women from Tunisia, in order to finally infect and destroy all of them.

 These women were so sick that licensed brothels in some countries wouldn't allow them to work after their checkup.

Hours before they start their work, they were brought to an abandoned house in the middle of the way to have them change their clothes to jilbab and burqa. The women changed their appearance shortly like

Arab women. They were told that the Muslim fighters don't like to see women without hijab.

In the bus terminus near the border of Syria, when the rebel group leaders saw the buses carrying women, they rushed toward them. Each of them were trying hard to gain some women to bring them to his jihadi group. The leader from Abu Bakr's group quickly reached one of those buses and texted his boss that he had seized one of those buses full of women.

"Choose two of the best for Abu Bakr, but they should not be blonde" Abu Hajar replied him. He believed according to Sunnah, blonde women were rejected by the prophet of Islam, so they are loathed.

The leader moved toward the women to perform his superior's orders. He removed the borqa off their faces one by one to see their face and their eyes. To mark the chosen ones, he made a hole in the corner of their burqa. The women didn't say a word, because it would have been revealed that they are not Arab and that might have caused problems.

On the way, the bus arrived to an inspection station which belonged to another Islamist rebel group. It was ridiculous. Tens Of Islamist groups were armed and formed rebel groups and was fighting against the government. Everyone claimed being revolutionist.

The bus stopped slowly. The leader was a little frightened. Because the women might have been seized. A rebel fighter who had worn a mask approached the bus. "Who are these women?" he asked.

-"Some fighters who are going to fight."

-"I have to search them."

He started searching the passengers. After groping them, he got out of the bus. "Get out of the bus, all of you. You are arrested," he ordered them.

Some masked Arab men came to the bus with their guns to evacuate the bus. The Abu Bakr's leader demanded to talk to the head of the group but in response he received a gun stock. The leader and the bus driver were jailed in a horrible hole. The leader had passed out so they dragged them on the ground.

The commander of the group intended to give those women to his own men. That night the women were swung between the men. The men was thinking it was a feast and it would give them more strength and motivation for coming days.

The next day the leader and the bus driver were released without the women. "Now you can go to hell," the commander told them.

They moved back to the bus terminus on the border of Syria with Turkey. The driver was so angry that he dropped the leader before reaching the destination. "You bring me bad luck," he told the leader.

Leader got out and the bus rapidly left that place. Leader decided to wait in the terminus until he can find another group of the women of Nikah.

***

In the regions under the control of Abu Bakr, in Aleppo and Ar-Raqqah the complete Islamic laws were executed. One day, after reading some pages of Islam history, Abu Bakr decided to announce Islamic State in the regions under his domination. His model was the prophet of Islam who established an Islamic government 14 centuries ago in the lands he had conquered.

Abu Bakr announced a statement emphasizing the establishment of the Islamic State of Iraq and Levant, so executing the Islamic laws were obligatory in the occupied regions. He also called himself an Islam caliph. Beside this instruction, he made a historical symmetry sampling. He ordered to destroy all historical symbols like statues and places which were thousands of years old. He had symbolized his act as the prophet's action in destroying idols and places for idolatry.

Islamic State's domination in historical sites in Aleppo had made an illegitimate source of income, museums were being plundered and tens of statues were destroyed or shot.

One day while Abu Bakr was evaluating the advance of his men toward Damascus, suddenly an idea came to his mind. He noticed his stupid imagination about destroying the historical monuments was only depriving him of millions of dollars of money. He called Abu Hajar. "Tell the fighters that they aren't allowed to destroy any other monument from this moment," he told him.

"They are the symbols of unawareness. Why did you decide this?" Abu Hajar said while he was surprised.

"They value millions of dollars. We need money to run the Islamic government. You better go and find an antique dealer to sell them," Abu Bakr said.

Retarded mind of Abu Hajar couldn't understand this. "We destroy them for desire of God, just like the prophet did to idols when he conquered Mecca," he said.

When Abu Hajar left, Abu Bakr sat on his royal throne to review his historical notes one more time.

"I made a right decision about selling the statues. The prophet also used the benefits of seizing the properties of kafir merchants for jihad in God's path," he was saying to himself.

Then he moved toward the map installed on the wall and marked the oil lands with a red marker. "And it is so that God make his servants wealthy. Whenever I sell oil, I wouldn't be worried about the money anymore," he said.

He noted some points on the walls of his residency: tax levied on non-Muslims, extortion of the ones who pretended to be Muslims but were not in heart, selling oil, the financial aids from sheikhs of Persian Gulf countries.

He didn't find a paper so he found a piece of fabric and wrote the appointment order of the Islamic State's treasurer. He purposed Abu Salah for this position. He was the man in charge of plunders from the Shiite shrines in Iraq. Abu Bakr immediately called him to manage the income and expenditure of the Islamic state.

Abu Bakr did one more important work. He prepared an announcement and ordered to use the word of Ghazw for all of the military operations. Ghazw was the word used for the wars in which the prophet was the commander. He knew himself the successor of prophet in this century and he wanted vitalize the image of Islam in 1400 years ago.

***

There was a real mess in the region where the prostitute women were seized. The fighters in contact of ill women were suffering from painful diseases and the non-stop irritation and itch on their penis wouldn't leave them even for a second. The situation was so disordered that a complete battalion, put down their guns and rushed to health centers in Turkey. Therefore a vast area was out of the control of the rebels. Sick women ran away when they saw the situation like this.

12

Sexual Jihad uninterrupted

In the following days the Tunisian women finally
arrived. The spies didn't succeed in their plans, so now
it was the turn of jihadi women to serve the jihadist
fighters by a religious fatwa.

The women from Tunis divided between three groups:
Abu Bakr's men, al-Nusra rebels and the Free Syrian
Army forces. They were totally 120 women. The
women did their best to be in a good condition and
they were nourished with dates and pineapples. It was
terrifying, 120 women for thousands of fighters. They
couldn't see the catastrophe. They were joyful with
the promise of heaven. The fighters also were
dreaming of heaven. Totally everything ended in
heaven.

The women were divided at the well-known terminus on the border of Turkey and Syria. After the division, 35 women were the share of Abu Bakr's Islamic State. These women were brought to a camp near Aleppo. Abu Bakr was supposed to visit them in person and probably choose some for himself.

The women were wearing niqab and were fully covered. They prayed first. Their behavior was completely spiritual. There were virgin girls amongst them who were completely calm.

Abu Bakr entered the camp with a masked face accompanied by armed fighters.

The women said hello in deep Arabic accent. Abu Bakr replied them. "I want a girl to be my partner in Nikah," he said.

The women were silent. "I am ready for everything in the way of Islam targets," one of them suddenly said.

Abu Bakr sent one of his bodyguards to inspect the woman. He removed the niqab off her face. She had black eyes and her face was beautiful.

The guard confirmed, "You go with me," Abu Bakr addressed woman.

The day after, the Nikah started and the fighters made queues with their tokens in specific places .

A Saudi medicine was always present to avoid any problems. The sex service were available from 8 p.m. to 2 a.m. According to Islam Nikah was forbidden during the day. After one or two nights there were scratches on men's faces. Apparently they behaved so brutally during their sex. Some of them were so greed or violent during their time with women that women had no choice but to attack them and scratch their ugly disgusting faces.

When a weak passed from the time the women of Nikah entered, there were good advances in the battle fields. The Islamic State group proceeded in some points in Aleppo. Al-Nusra had Homs almost under its control. In some regions, their progress interfered the movements of the Free Syrian Army, but they finally agreed on their positions.

The Nikah fever had spread in Arab countries, In Saudi

Arabia some families were ready to send their daughters to Syria because of the real faith they had in jihad.

Omm e Salme was one of those girls sent to Syria for Nikah with his father's full propensity. "My desire is to fulfill the jihadists' needs," she told her mother while she was packing her suitcase.

"I will return with a baby in my belly and grow him up to be a fighter." she continued.

"Such a pity that I am old," her mother replied, "There is nothing more worthy than fighting with kafirs for God. You made us and your clan proud."

"I will pray for you in Kaaba to have twins," her father said while he was on the verge of tears, "And I hope they would be fighters if they are boys, or be in Nikah with fighters like you if they were girls."

Most of people in Arab peninsula thought like Omm e Salme and her family. They believed helping jihadis in Syria is like a worship that fades their sin and clear their path to heaven.

In Homs and Aleppo the women of Nikah slept with 20 to 25 fighters every other night. The Salafi muftis didn't have any fatwa in order to predict what must be done if the women became pregnant.

Gradually there were the signs of pregnancy in women. The Saudi medicine permitted ten to fifteen more intercourses for pregnant women.

Omm e Salme after joining the jihadist women appeared more active than others and tried to compensate other women's inactivity. She did ghusl before every intercourse and had deep faith in what she was doing.

The women rested during the day when the men were in battle field. Gradually the number of pregnant women increased and it was the time to return home to give birth to their children.

The fighters were unsatisfied with women leaving. They expected more fresh women to come which needed vaster calls and religious setting.

They insisted the muftis must issue more fatwas to persuade more women to come to Syria for Nikah.

Though women tried to spend more time with fighters before leaving them. Omm e Salme was more persistent than others and wouldn't stop for a second. She believed a gold castle is made in heaven for her for each intercourse she gives the fighters. The Nikah was going to end and women were returning home. The pregnant women had to be with their families or husbands to be cared. Even the thought was foolish that a husband receives his woman pregnant from a stranger man. But apparently there was no alternative. Husbands and fathers believed the children from their wives or daughters are the future fighters and jihadis for Islam.

With reduction in number of women for Nikah there were some problems in the Islamist fighters' progress toward Damascus. The amount of casualties started to grow. The Free Syrian army had less advance though they acted more orderly. Their political backup group, The Syrian National Council was trying hard to lobby with European governments to gain their military intervention in Syria as they did in Libya.

The soldiers from the Free Syrian Army were counting

the moments to occupy Damascus but their progress was far from expectations. Russia and Iran were firmly supporting Assad while United States and NATO didn't have more money to maintain for vast attacks in Syria.

13

Ominous travel in the middle of blood and smoke

Abu Bakr al-Baghdadi had announced Islamic State in districts under his control and executed the law of Sharia. Al-Nusra and other small jihadist groups also did the same in their captured areas.

The beautiful city of Aleppo became a ruin during only some months. The buildings had collapsed and the doors were laid on the ground. The tramp dogs looking for a piece of bone were sometimes shot by fighters for fun.

Atrocity, obscenity and hatred had spread in Aleppo, Homs and other cities of Syria and the monster of adversity and depravity had landed all over the country and any exit from that miserable situation seemed impossible.

The propaganda part of the Islamic State of Abu Bakr had announced a vast call on the internet to abstract fighters. Joining this group specially for young Arab people who didn't have a job or money in their own countries, seemed interesting. The young Arab who had immigrated to European countries felt humiliation and rejection and they looked for a chance to escape this tedious situation. They bought the ticket of turkey on their own or in a group to go and join the fighters in the battle field.

A limited number of European and American citizens who had become bored of the order, law, welfare and quiet in their lives, found it pretty interesting to participate in a real war and experience the crime and murder they always had seen in movies and video games.

Paul, Andre and Monica went to an Islamic charity center in the center of London on a working day after the weekend. The Islamic center secretly attracted volunteers for jihad in Syria. But these three young volunteers weren't Muslim so they weren't qualified.

The man in charge of registration was a strong man with bald head and long beard who was chatting online with someone in Syria. He explained these three guys condition to the one on the other side of the line.

The person in Syria asked for some minutes to talk to someone with a higher rank.

Abu Bakr had sat in his room when Abu Hajar entered. "Right now they have informed me that there are some young kafirs from Europe who are volunteer to join us in Syria," he said.

Abu Bakr went to his notes to find the rule for the situation. According to this rule kafirs were well behaved by the prophet of Islam in order to be attracted to Islam. So their hearts would be towards this religion and the finally would become Muslims.

"Tell them to come," Abu Bakr said without any hesitation, "They will convert to Islam with no doubt and they will fight for us."

"Ask them why they want to come to Syria." Abu Hajar texted the charity responsible in London.

The young were asked. "The act of the fighters is interesting for us." Paul said.

"Which act is interesting for you?" Abu Hajar wouldn't accept easily.

"Decapitation and killing the opponents," this time Andre answered.

Abu Hajar was finally satisfied. "Manage their dispatch," he ordered the registration responsible.

The man who had found a good chance to mooch the young volunteers asked them some money for helping the fighters. Then he got their cell phones to install some applications of religious speeches and preaching. He insisted listening them multiple times per day in order to be prepared mentally.

In Germany, a Turk football player named Founak was living in a big house with his wife and children in complete peace and elegance. Pool, sauna, so much money, reputation and pride they all made him have a nice family life in Europe.

But he suddenly changed under the affects of Salafi Islamists. He couldn't concentrate enough on his matches. Lack of motivation made him sit on the substitute bench and loose his fitness.

There was a bad virus in his mind. He was ready to leave this heaven on earth to another vague heaven.

One day he finally announced his foolish decision. "We'll return to Turkey," he said to his wife and children. " I want to join the jihadist fighters."

His wife Marita strongly refused but it was useless.

"Do you know the meaning of jihad for Allah?" he asked his wife, "What is the value of this welfare and quiet life while the right and the truth is being disrespected?"

"I've heard if anyone sacrifices his world's convenience, he would be given a better life in the other world." he continued.

"Which fool does so for something that is not assured?" his wife answered angrily.

Founak was getting so mad at his wife finding her like a kafir merited to be killed. "If you continue I would be obliged to execute the command of god," he yelled, "so please shut up!"

He made an Islamic appearance for himself under the supervision of a salafi mufti. His shaved face was replaced by long beard. he only shaved his moustache and he became like Arab clergymen.

Founak bought the tickets to Turkey without informing his club and got ready to join the jihadists in Syria.

They arrived in Istanbul early in the morning. His face was so silly that no one could recognize him. No moustache, long beard, bald head, just like muftis!

Fear and discontent was obvious in his wife's face. "What shall we do, these children and I when you go to Syria?" she told her changed husband.

The man's solution was foolish. "You'll go to refugee camps in the border."

"You are insane." she said, "What the hell shall we do there?"

"You have to tolerate difficulties for God," he said zealously.

"From a villa in Germany to the wet and damp tents on the border," she said insanely, "Your thoughts are so wrecked that I'm sure I can't change this path to misery."

They were going toward the border by bus and the man was torturing the woman with religious advices he gave her. Sometimes he threatened her with a calm annoying voice. Even he hit her head to the bus window, "When a woman stands in front of Sharia, she must be punished."

When they arrived in border his wife and children were delivered by camp to be settled. Founak was excited to fight sooner. He let them with no hesitation and introduced himself to a go-between from al-Nusra group. Everything was arranged and he was rapidly transferred to a far spot in Syria.

They passed a road in a Toyota pickup with two other men. The more they proceeded they could hear the fighter planes more loudly. They were under the gunshot. A fighter started shooting towards the sky. Some moments later a rocket was shot and Founak and his two accompaniers turned into dust in some seconds. His folly turned to a disaster so soon and before he could hold a gun.

***

The Syrians who were under the fighters' control became their puppets so rapidly because of their thoughts and cultural poverty. The Sunni tribes who had pledged allegiance to the rebel because of fear or dissatisfaction, had to act as they wanted to the end.

The group of Abu Bakr was really sensitive to tribes pledging allegiance otherwise they would kill them with no hesitation. In one case the head of the tribe was asked to send a girl to Abu Bakr as a present.

The head of the tribe considered Marjae, his niece as the present for Abu Bakr. Marjae was completely resisting this horrible suggestion. Her uncle finally called for her and threatened her to be stoned if she didn't accept it. Marjae was in a hard situation. The tribe council held a meeting to decide on issues like her virginity. They decided to ask a boy from the tribe to have the honor to remove her virginity before handing her in.

Marjae had confronted a terrible decision. Again she resisted but her uncle told if she didn't accept, the whole tribe would be killed by Abu Bakr's men. She was supposed to announce her acceptance as soon as possible. She finally accepted unpleasantly and they arranged to hold a big tent two days prior to her delivery to jihadis and marry her to the mentioned boy in a weird ceremony. They entered the tent after the wedding while a big crowd from the tribe had surrounded them. The crowd was supposed to cheer up when the bride and the groom left the tent and it was over meaning that the boy had removed the virginity of Marjae.

The tribe people were happy. But Marjae had a more terrible decision. she had placed some explosive capsules in her body which would explode by any contact. Some minutes past and the crowd got closer and closer to the tent. Some naughty curious children had brought their heads inside the tent to see what was going on. Suddenly a massive explosion took place and a wall of fire and smoke shaped. The tent burnt for hours with the people inside and around it.

***

The group of the European boys and girls who had registered through a charity center in London entered the Istanbul airport at the promised dey with their tablets and a backpack full of food supplies. A Turk go-between delivered them and brought them to the border of Syria on a private car.

It was almost getting dark when they arrived the border. Because of the darkness and insecure situation of the cities near the border, they were brought to a safe house inside a rather ruined village.

The Turk agent informed his men in the Abu Bakr's jihadist group that everything is arranged. The village house was like a crypt. He had decided to take Monica to another place but the boys objected. "I think they are just bunch of fools," Paul told his friends in a frightened tone when the agent went away, "I hope the fighters to be less fool than him."

They were so exhausted and they fell asleep but they woke up in the middle of the night by suspicious voices. They saw shadows outside the street which carried big packages into a truck.

"I think these are weapons," Monica said.

"SShh! They shouldn't notice that we understand it," Andre said.

The moving shadows outside were talking to each other in a Turkish accent. It was nearly the sunrise time when the noisy shipment finished. They were getting ready to sleep when suddenly a step was heard outside the door.

The door was opened. They pretended they were slept. "Get ready! It's time to go," the man at the door said in English.

One of the boys who had forgotten his role as being slept reacted immediately. "But we were supposed to leave in the morning," he said.

"We are informed that the routes are safe now and the midway traps have been removed. We are just three hours to the destination," the man said.

It was still dark when they entered the back part of the truck. "Sit beside the boxes and don't move. It is dangerous," the man said.

The door was closed and the truck moved. "Imagine that we are going to pass the Germans' inspection station in some minutes," Monica told her friends excitedly.

"We are done then. Help mummy!" Paul said in an irony way.

"We must be armed at the moment to protect ourselves," Andre said.

The truck stopped an hour later. There were odd voices outside. A man with a deep Arabic accent was saying something to the driver. The engine was shut off and the sounds were more clear. An Arab fighter's rough voice could be heard. The young boys and girl quickly hid behind the ammo boxes. The back door was opened. Monica was right. It was the inspection station of one of the tens lawless jihadi groups.

An Arab with a red mask looked inside the truck and he saw the boxes piled up. The young guys couldn't be seen. The door was shut. After some seconds the engine started and the truck moved.

"We are in a desert now. It is like the scene of the Lawrence of Arabia," one of the boys said, "I bet if we could see outside the window, we would see some camels with a Bedouin who passes across the desert."

After two more hours finally the truck reached its destination. The door was opened and the Turk go-between asked the kids to get out of the truck. There was the camp of Abu Bakr's men. Some masked Arabs were unloading the ammo boxes.

They were delivered to another Arab who could speak fluent English. That man separated Monica from the others and brought her to an unknown place.

The boys got angry. "Here is the military area and disobeying is not accepted," the Arab man said in a rough accent. The boys were taken into a hot tent in the middle of the camp. It took about half an hour till Monica showed up. She was somehow disturbed. "These fools are sexually sick. Ten ugly stinky fighter attacked me. Fortunately I took my medicine immediately." she said as soon as she returned to her friends.

"I think we are caught," a boy said angrily.

"We would be so lucky if they don't come to us for their dirty intentions," Paul said.

The Arab go-between arrived and they got quiet. "You will be transferred to a villa house to make some rest," the man said.

They got on a Toyota and passed the occupied districts. Gunfire was heard. "What is going on here?" one of the boys asked.

"It is war inside the city and everything may happens" the Arab man said.

They entered a ruin street in Aleppo. They were shocked by the scenes they were seeing. Monica just forgot what had happened to her some minutes ago. They were surprised by those ruins. Headless bodies and cut hands and feet were in every corner of the pavement.

The car entered a rather quiet district and stopped by a two stage building. They were accompanied into the building. There were holes in the walls which seemed to be embedded for the guns to check outside.

They were settled on the first floor. A tray was brought to them with bread, dates and a jar of milk. They asked about the internet access. "Everything is available, even hot shower," the Arab man said, "but be careful not to touch that girl. Otherwise you would be whipped."

There was cameras and microphone inside the room. They were completely under control.

***

There was strict Islamic ruling in the districts occupied by Islamic fighters. The Sharia executive agents didn't have any free time. Detention and whipping sentences were issued one after another. Ayman al-Zawahiri, the leader of al-Qaeda messaged Abu Bakr to continue the Taliban governing pattern in order to ease the execution of Sharia later in Damascus and Baghdad.

"Remember that the borders of our domination is throughout the world and Europe and America will be one day under our domination," al-Zawahiri said.

One day the Arab man came to the new European jihadists to take them to the city for watching the execution of Sharia. They rapidly got ready. Monica was excited as she was going to watch a thriller movie.

"It couldn't be better than this," Paul said.

They went with the same Toyota pickup. They were given cotton clothes to cover their faces. They passed some ruined streets and reached a big square. Two women were supposed to be whipped. One of them was Khaledeh who had buried some men inside a hole in her house. She was caught once more and apparently this time she didn't have a way out.

They were brought to a high stage which was made like the execution stages in sixteenth century. A female executioner made them bend. A fighter started whipping them while he was holding a book under his arm. After the fifth lash strike, blood appeared on their back. Khaledeh used bad language. So the judge increased the number of lashes. The foreigners were staring this mercilessness. "What have they done that they deserve this sentence?" one of the girls asked.

"One of them were in the street without a Mahram and the other one was caught while chatting with a shopkeeper," their guide explained.

"What is a Mahram?" They all asked.

"A man with a blood relationship, like father, brother or uncles," he explained.

The women were taken to the checkup room to be examined by a special agent to make sure that they had been properly flogged so that the lashes had made them bleeding.

There was a bloody line on the back of Khaledeh but the other woman had only shallow bruises, so the judge ordered five more lashes for her.

Some moments after these two women, two boys were brought with shackled hands and blindfolded eyes. The judge announced their crime as listening to forbidden music. The young foreigners asked the reason and they were shocked to know the answer.

"What is the amusement in Islam then?" Paul asked while they were returning from the ritual.

"Going to mosque, pray, Salat, Jihad and martyrdom," the Arab answered being surprised of the question.

Monica had no good memory of Arab horny men. "And also abusing the women," she added.

"The Muslim women don't consider it abusing," Arab man replied, "They are the kindness and affection giving to women by the men."

"Hasn't your enthusiasm increased today after seeing these sides of Islam?" the Arab man continued.

"Ah, We'll convert to Islam sooner than you would imagine after seeing all of these beautiful things," one of the boys answered ironically.

The Arab man took them home and promised to bring them to see beheading for the next day.

The fighter planes noises wouldn't stop even for a second and it seemed so normal. They all had laid in a corner of the room surfing the net on their phones. The fighters started to shoot the planes with their guns senselessly. One of those young boys ran to the window. "Hey kids! A funny insane is shooting the airplanes," he told to his friends.

They started the mockery. "The plane would crash in a moment," Monica said. "What do you think of throwing stones the those fighter planes?" Andre continued. As they were joking a massive thunder started and a whistle was being heard. It was like something very big or a rocket was getting close to the earth. Everything had been thrown in the air, suddenly the ceiling tumbled down and fire and smoke filled the room.

After some days none of the fighters went after those kids. It was common in the areas under the control of the fighters to leave the dead in the ruins.

14

bull-headed killers

The advance of the Abu Bakr's forces toward Damascus was so slow and with lots of casualties. They encountered heavy defense with lots of explosive traps. Abu Hajar was assigned by Abu Bakr to make a contact with the head of a violent gang in Morocco and ask them for some bull-headed errant Arab who kill others easily. The go-between who spoke with a harsh unclear voice was named Abu Shomar. "The bull-headed men want money. Can you pay them?" he asked.

"Aren't they interested in jihad?" Abu Hajar asked.

"Their profession is murder and massacre," Abu Shomar said, "they are fed up with the nonsense about hell and heaven. Do you understand?"

Abu Hajar paused the conversation to ask for Abu Bakr's opinion. He went to his boss resort to consult him. When he entered Abu Bakr's room he found his wife from Nikah in an inappropriate position. The woman didn't mention the situation, put on the burqa and started talking to Abu Hajar while her hands were naked and her feet were in a tempting position. Abu Bakr returned from the rest room. "What is going on?" He asked his assistant.

Abu Hajar who intended to get close to the woman suddenly got interrupted. "I talked to an insane mannamed Abu Shomar. He said the hired bull-headed killers ask for money in return of fighting." he said.

"You should have told him there is no more precious reward than heaven," Abu Bakr said while drying his hands with a towel.

"They don't believe in such things," he replied with a smirk, "they get paid to kill."

"There is no other choice," Abu Bakr said, "Ask him to send some of them over, we would pay them."

Abu Hajar made another contact to Abu Shomar some hours later and asked him for some of his insane bull-headed men.

"They kill people as easy as drinking water," the go-between said, "They can destroy any monster. They just want their money weekly in cash."

"Why do they need money when they might die every second?" Abu Hajar wanted to be smart.

"Listen you fool coward!" Abu Shomar answered angrily, "If you want your head and your boss's head to be a lesson for Syrians, stop paying them."

After some days Abu Shomar arranged a meeting with merciless criminals who had been just released from jail in Morocco in a horrific port in Casablanca. The invited men were dark faced Arabs who were so powerful and also irritable. Ten criminals each one leading a gang of twenty gangsters, came to the meeting which was held on the deck of a wrecked ship.

While Abu Shoamr was talking to them about their mission, the gangsters only concentrated on the next puff of their cigarettes and they also sometimes played with the pebbles on the deck. One of them described how he had exploded a school with all of its students when he was in Benghazi, Libya for the last time. And he had accused the government of Gaddafi so easily.

"The revolutionists called me and suggested a very good money to explode a cinema while all the visitors were inside," another one said, "my main mission was to defame the regime. And everyone blamed the government so easily. No one even asked why a government must kill its people while they are watching a movie."

"O.K. It's enough to tell the stories," Abu Shomar said after he heard their records, "Everything is arranged, you are going to be delivered on the border of Turkey."

"Hey! What about the money?" a criminal said nervously.

"They pay weekly, in dollars," Abu Shomar replied.

"Are we only hired to kill?"

"Yes. By sickle, sword, gun, whatever you can. And by the way, they say you'll go to heaven if you get killed."

"Shut Up! The bastards think we are some children. We've heard these things a lot. No one goes to heaven from hell."

"Do your job. You are not going to discuss some religious villains."

***

A week later they arrived in the border of Turkey as supposed and they were delivered by the leaders sent by Abu Bakr and were brought to the camp by bus via a tortuous road.

"We are hungry and tired and we want food," a gangster shouted when he got bored on the way.

"We'll be in the camp in ten minutes," An Arab replied frightened.

The opposing man got quiet and looked at his watch. He was keeping the time like a referee in a football match to start a fuss if they didn't arrived soon. In less than half an hour the bus turned in a sidetrack, they reached the camp and the bell-headed men started taking the needed courses for the coming missions.

***

15

Pointless Battle in City Center

Gradually with the situation getting more critical, the militant groups got closer to the gate of Damascus step by step. The forces from al-Nusra, the Khorasanis, Ansar ul-Islam, Free Syrian Army, Abu Bakr's group, Syrian Islamic Front, Ahrar ash-Sham and some other terrorist groups had increased their pressure to enter Damascus and capture the capital.

The Syrian army resisted hardly and progress toward the center of Damascus was very hard as an Iranian commander had planned the resistance. But finally the defend lines of army broke in the south of the city and the fighters from al-Nusra and Free Army followed by the trained militants of Abu Bakr al-Baghdadi could reach the streets in the south of Damascus.

In this situation almost 95 percent of Syria was out of the control of government and a final pressure could easily terminate everything.

In this chaos, Bashar al-Assad was indifferently visiting his patients in his modern equipped clinic in the north of Damascus when he was contacted by the presidential guard. "Mr. president the terrorists has broken into the defend line in south of the capital and they are proceeding," a high-ranked commander reported with a shaky tone.

Bashar ordered to let the programs of the radio and television continue ordinarily as if nothing had happened. "We shall not scare the people by no means," he said, "Call General Kassim and ask him what to do."

Kassim was completely aware of everything. He had started his actions when he saw the dangerous situation before he was called by governmental authorities as he had full power to make every decision. He sent a battalion of five hundred men to protect the presidential palace, Radio and Television and Sayyidah Zaynab Mosque. The forces diffused in strategic points.

It was getting more and more tricky. The gunfire could be heard around the television broadcasting center.

Kassim ordered an Iranian commander to situate in the basement, parking and inside the restrooms of the television building. The TV was amazingly showing its regular programs while viewers could hear the sound of gunfire and explosions.

With the initiative of Kassim and some Syrian expert commanders five lines of fire named melting wall formed from Sayyidah Zaynab Mosque to essential government centers.

There was a heavy pressure made by Free Army to penetrate to city center. At the same time al-Nusra fighters were getting close to city center. Also Abu Bakr's militants were proceeding in some points like Dummer.

Abu Bakr had set those bull-headed gangsters from Morocco on a mission to occupy the Sayyidah Zaynab Mosque in the chaos. He intended to explode the mosque and believed by doing so the Iranians base would have been weakened and this mental stroke would break them and they would stop supporting Assad, so the fall of Damascus would be easier.

The Free Army had intensified their pressure to reach the presidential palace but their advance was slow and with lots of casualties. A soldier with a walkie-talkie accompanying a commander from the Free army survived a dreadful battle and escaped into a ruin where was used by fighters as trench. The commander contacted the control center in the border of Turkey and Syria. "By tomorrow evening it's over," he reported his superior while panting.

The man in the control post immediately contacted General Izgled and reported him the last news from the front line. Izgled happily contacted Penter's office in Jeddah. His Assistant told him that he has gone to mosque for his religious practice and would return in some hours.

After saying his prayers Penter returned and was informed of unbelievable advances of jihadis. He soon called his Qatarian friend and suggested an urgent meeting in Istanbul. "It is almost over. Let's get together to arrange a victory ceremony," Penter told him. The members of Syrian National Council also held an urgent meeting to form the cabinet. "Gentlemen! now on consider yourselves the ministers. The government will be ours in coming days," the head of this group told his men after organizing the transitional government.

The condition was getting worse and worse in Damascus. Kassim, the Iranian general asked the telecommunication company of Damascus to cut all the lines in order to prevent wiring their conversations. He also asked the professional engineers from Hezbollah of Lebanon based in Syria to maintain a secure communication network for him and the presidential guard. They had disturbed the telecommunication network in Israel and had wired them before. After some hours the secure communication line for Kassim and the presidential guard was ready. Kassim called President Assad in person. The contact was hardly made but he finally succeeded to talk to president. "Mr. President! A personal jet will land in the palace area in some hours and it will take you and your family members to a secure place," Kassim told him.

"I can't leave Damascus. But you can take my family," Assad said.

"We can arrange everything without your presence," Kassim said, "There is nothing to worry."

Assad had a logical reason for not leaving. "It won't give a positive feedback to the nation. I want to make a TV statement from my palace to my people."

An Arab channel released the news about Assad and his family escaping from Damascus. Bashar Assad appeared on TV and talked to the people of Syria from his room in the presidential palace. "By god will we will defeat the enemies of this country," he said.

Assad insured the people that everything is under the control of the government and the gunfire and explosions heard, shows the resistance of the nation young men who fight terrorists.

This message couldn't cause any trouble in fighters progress. The Arabic news agencies analogized it with the presence of Qaddafi between people while Tripoli was falling. He went among people to assure them that everything is normal but he had reached the end line.

The bull-headed men of Abu Bakr succeeded to reach inside of the Sayyidah Zaynab Mosque. Their attack was so well-managed that the Iranian defenders of the mosque were taken unawares and a number of them were killed and Abu Bakr's bull-headed men got the control of the shrine. They evacuated the bodies, ruined some tombs and did inappropriate things.

The situation was not good at all. The fall of the mosque where was the basemen of the Iranian forces made the fighters to underestimate the power of the Iranians. When Kassim was informed about losing the mosque he quickly rushed from the borderline of Lebanon to Damascus. He rapidly sent a skilled group of his commandos to reclaim the mosque. But it wasn't that easy.

The bull-headed killers had placed dynamites and explosives inside the mosque. They seemed completely cool like they were just replacing a light bulb or fastening bolts and nuts.

Abu Bakr was personally monitoring the operation. He told Abu Hajar to remind the head of the bull-headed men to bring out the bodies of respected Shiite clergies from their tombs and set them on fire.

Abu Hajar made a contact to their head on walkie-talkie. "Abu Bakr wants the bodies of respected Shiite clergies exhumed and set on fire," he told.

"We have done it before you even open your mouth," the head said, "Send us some experienced fighters to protect the area around the shrine till we are arranging to explode here."

This conversation was enough for the Iranians to set up a plan. The commandos who were moving toward the shrine immediately changed their appearance and planned to introduce themselves as Abu Bakr fighters wearing the Arab clothes and masking their faces. The Iranians spoke fluent Arabic, so they immediately arrived in mosque and pretended to be the guards who were supposed to protect the shrine.

Five Iranian commandos who had disguised like Abu Bakr's men entered the mosque. "What the hell do you do here?" The head of the bull-headed men who looked like a monster said in an angry vile tone.

"We are the aid forces you had asked," one of the Iranians answered.

The wicked monster had suspected the situation. He tried to make a contact to Abu Hajar. One of the commandos noticed and immediately started a kit which would make all the wireless connections impossible. The head who was a little confused and nervous gave up the contact with Abu Hajar after giving him a swearword.

"We are placing a bomb here," he said to commandos, "look around and don't let anyone get close to us."

The Iranians played their role very well. The subversives were working like mice with the walls of the mosque and were trying to make holes as big as a handheld radio to place the bombs while cutting or adding wires.

The Iranian commandos were prowling around the subversives. "Don't get so close, you'll bother us. Just be careful no one comes around." one of them told the commandos.

The commandos changed their way and pretended they are obeying fighters who act exactly as they are ordered by their superiors. Placing the bombs was almost done when commandos went to the bombers. Each of those Iranians were holding a small piece like an AA Battery, they showed it to them. "When we were in Afghanistan, we used these parts to increase the power of the explosion." they said.

"How do you know it works?" one of those monsters said.

"These are the supplementary for detonators. We have stolen them from NATO in Afghanistan. They work 3 seconds after the explosion leaving nothing." they replied.

They believed the trick and took the supplementary part from them. As soon as they touched those tools they fell on the ground. The commandos acted rapidly and neutralized the bombs. The mosque was completely under the control of Iranians while they were in the fighters' costume.

All those bull-headed gangsters diminished so quietly and at the same time the forces of Abu Bakr arrived whom were asked to dispatch by a demand on walkie-talkie. The Iranians overcame them as easy as drinking water.

The battles went on in the center of Damascus. A group of militants from the Free Army and al-Nusra were trying to occupy the television broadcasting building. The leaders of The Syrian National Council outside Syria had prepared a statement to declare the fall of the government and announce the new political system and it was supposed to be read after occupying the TV Station by a high-ranked Free Army General.

The defense wall of Assad's army finally broke under the ultimate pressure of the fighters and they found their way inside the building of the governmental radio and television station. The TV of Damascus was broadcasting its regular programs. There were some communication experts among the fighters who were aware of technical issues of broadcasting systems. The Iranians commandos were hiding with Kassim in the garage and the restrooms of the building.

The invaders easily reached the sixth floor, where the programs were released live. Some fighters entered the pre-casting room. There was a heavy gunfire. Two generals who had entered the pre-casting room shot the two employees working there. Now it was the time to enter the live broadcasting room where could be seen by people all around Syria.

The invading general hesitated a lot more than he should and was preparing himself to go on the air assuming that everything was over and he just had to go inside and read the statement. After some minutes weird voices could be heard from outside the room. Suddenly some commandos covered in black broke into the room. In some seconds a fusillade of bullets and grenades filled the room. The general and his comrades were defeated in some seconds. The sound could be easily heard in the program which was on air at the moment.

The TV show host who was a beautiful young lady said: "Dear viewers! This bruit is the effort of our nation soldiers to punish the terrorists."

After cleaning the room an Iranian commando pushed the door a little open and made a gesture showing that everything is under control and there is nothing to worry about.

In the lower floors of the building the fight still went on. Some attackers with their explosive vests were trying to penetrate into the sensitive points. Two suicide attackers exploded themselves in the middle of the commandos. some Iranian commandos and the army soldiers were killed. After each man's explosion another one would come forward. They hadn't made a long way when they were all blockaded by plenty of commandos and placed under the heavy gunfire.

They were almost completely destroyed. Kassim made contact on a special covering line to the presidential guard and asked forces to clean the areas around the building.

***

In a fancy hotel in Istanbul, Penter, the senior Qatarian authority and General Izgled were waiting the second to second report of the mission which led to Assad's fall. The last report given to them was entering the TV building. Penter was extremely happy.

"Now on we must think of rebuilding the cities after war," the Qatarian man said who assumed everything over.

"Tell the conquering commanders of Damascus that we want Assad alive," Penter reminded Izgled .

"Calm down Mr. Penter," the Turk general replied, "As I have been told it will be over in some hours, we are going to pick the fruit of the people's revolution."

There was a voice coming out of the walkie-talkie and all three of them ran toward it. A commander from the Free Syrian Army was on the line. "Our forces were eradicated at the building of the TV and Radio broadcasting," he said in a shaky voice and nervous tone.

Penter passed out and fell on the ground. His Qatarian friend helped him to go and lay on the sofa.

"You are some incapable idiots. How can it happen when you had entered the building?" General Izgled said while he still couldn't believe this catastrophe.

"We were finishing the job when suddenly invisible commandos appeared everywhere and they fired at us from every corner," the commander replied on a short delay, "We were almost turning the door knob to the live performance room when they attacked us."

Penter broke down by hearing these words and started swearing Iranians. Izgled called an equipped hospital in Istanbul and arranged to transfer Penter to that hospital.

Penter wouldn't stop swearing even for a second. The Qatarian authority was by his side and was trying to console him.

Izgled brought up an interesting suggestion. "We may ask for help in this moment from NATO to hit the last strike. We need only a small push to finish everything," Izgled said, "you may use your influence on the political forces now Mr. Penter."

"Cancel the hospital," Penter said, "I will directly contact the United States embassy in Riyadh."

"Contact!" the Turk general said, "I'll arrange other things. We don't have much time and they should decide quickly."

Izgled called the VIP services of the foreign ministry and arranged everything on phone. Ten minutes later The United States ambassador in Riyadh called and started talking to Penter. Penter extremely insisted and emphasized on attacking Damascus and positions under the control of Assad by rockets from USA aerial fleet in Bahrain in order to ease the advance of the revolutionists.

The USA ambassador said that he had to ask about it from the White House. He was supposed to call back in fifteen minutes.

"These Americans don't even drink some water without the permission from Obama," Penter said.

Some minutes later the USA ambassador called. "Sir! Unfortunately the government of the United States doesn't know enough about the fighter groups in Damascus," he frankly said to Penter.

"They are our men," Penter said, "we have given the weapons you had sent us to these men."

"I mentioned all these matters to Mr. President," the ambassador said, "But he says we can't act without the agreement of the congress. The foreign minister also insisted that our duty is to support the democracy and we did it by reinforcing the revolutionists."

Penter hung up while swearing. "Nothing is clear yet," the Qatarian authority said to change the atmosphere, "Everything may turn in some hours for the good of the revolutionists. The conflict is not over yet. It all may finally lead to Assad's escape and occupying his palace by the protestors."

Izgled was very desperate. He called an authority in the prime minister office. "Sir, the dream of revival of Ottoman Empire is being failed," he said hopelessly.

The general with that thick moustache could hardly control his feelings. The one on the other side of the line was in a burst of profanity. "Send them auxiliary forces. What is this monkey business? I have exact information that Assad has escaped Damascus. Capturing the TV and radio building will be the last step." he said angrily to Izgled .

"We got forward to that point," Izgled said, "but the Iranians interfered and threw the revolutionists out of the building."

"Put those useless damned people on their places." the one on the phone screamed.

The phone was hung up and Izgled once more contacted the war front in Damascus. The connection failed and they finally decided to wait for their call.

Assad's presidential palace was under the strict control of the Iranians and the skilled presidential guards. A multi layer security belt was established around the palace and the TV and radio building. There was an important national security meeting in the ministry of security building. General Kassim was invited to the meeting but he said that the situation was so dangerous that he couldn't leave the palace even for a second. He sent an Iranian colonel on behalf of himself to the meeting.

The gunfire and explosion didn't stop even for a moment in Damascus. A mole in the national security council of Syria reported that the meeting was going to be held in the national security building. The commanders of al-Nusra and the Free Syrian Army planned an urgent operation. They sent a van full of explosives toward the national security building. The more terrible thing was that their conversations were wired and the operation room of the Free Army outside Damascus could directly hear their talks.

The meeting started. "Some of the army commanders has suggested to use chemical weapons in the conflicts with protestors," the head of the national security council said.

The Iranian colonel present at the meeting immediately refused this suggestion. "It is not a good decision at all," he said, "The invader forces are so close to the population centers that it may cause severe losses between civilians and that may lead to the intervention of UN security council."

The Syrian aerial forces commander disagreed too. "This idea is so stupid that can cause the United States and its allies to start a war against us," he said.

The Free Army military intelligence agents were listening to whatever was going inside the meeting. An intelligence agent quickly made a contact to Izgled and told him that they have received some important information.

"Something is going on. They have informed me important news are coming," Izgled told Penter who sat impatiently on the sofa.

"Oh God! Help us." Penter said and he was shocked.

In some minutes the details of the National Security Council meeting was reported completely to Izgled . Bringing up the issue of chemical weapons and then cancelling it brought a smile on Penter's face. "Be ready the stupid ambassador," he said ridiculously.

***

The sabotage center of the Free Army and al-Nusra which was tracking the conversations of the national security council meeting called a suicide van driver and told him to cautiously and quickly approach the Security department building in Damascus.

This conversation was being heard by the Iranians. Kassim was informed in Assad's palace and tried to make a contact with the security department in Damascus on the same covered line.

The argument had reached to important points when a guard officer rushed into the room without permission. "There is an urgent call for you," he told the Iranian colonel.

The colonel ran out of the room. "We have heard a suspicious conversation," Kassim told him, "A suicide van is moving toward a government establishment. Finish the meeting and leave the building right now."

The colonel ran back to the conference room. "Gentlemen! We are in danger. We must to leave this place sooner." he told the men in the meeting.

The operation room on the fighters' side noticed the urgent close of the session. They immediately called the suicide driver and told him hit the van blindly to the buildings around the target place. The suicide bomber became so agitated. He wetted his pants getting close to the moments of his death. The driver was a young man from Morocco who had joined the fighters for the promise of heaven. He increased his speed and once more controlled the clay guard he had put around his testis. The suicide bombers used to cover their penis with a protection to keep it safe during the explosion. They believed seconds after the explosion the beautiful women from heaven welcome them so an intact penis would be useful.

The meeting in the building of the security council was left unfinished and the present authorities used the emergency stairs to escape the building as soon as possible. The van had arrived near the building. The security guard were told to shoot RPG to any moving creature who was getting close to the building. The van appeared and the gunshot started. The van was targeted but the driver used a zigzag movement to avoid being hit. Finally he hit the van to parked cars near the building. There was a big explosion and fire and smoke covered everything. Just a few persons could escape and the other security agents were killed immediately.

In the operation room in Istanbul, Penter and his partners were waiting impatiently for the information from the meeting of the security authorities in Damascus. They received a message expressing the death of all present authorities in the security meeting in Damascus. They all screamed of happiness.

"I'm sure Kassim was in the meeting," Penter said, "His death means that the multi layer protection of Assad's palace would no longer exist and the revolutionists can have a plan for a new attack."

"We're not still sure about his assassination," Izgled said, "Has anyone confirmed his presence?"

The general made a contact to the Free Army intelligence center to make sure. The superior commander in charge of the center told him that an Iranian colonel was present in the meeting accompanied by an ordinary officer. In the middle of the meeting the colonel left because he had an important call and when he returned he asked everyone to leave the place. The colonel was killed in the attack.

The commander asked for some moments to investigate their spy in the security system of Syria to know about Kassim's status.

"He hasn't been killed," he replied after some minutes.

Penter knitted his brow. "It's better to bring up the subject of chemical bombs which was suggested in the meeting," Izgled said.

There were few battles around the presidential palace. Assad contacted the palace from an unknown place and asked his superior advisor to arrange another TV interview for him.

The advisor refused and told the president that he is not sure if it is a good decision in this situation.

"I'll be there in some minutes," Bashar said, "Prepare everything."

The superior advisor immediately informed Kassim. The helicopter carrying the president and his men landed in the palace some minutes later. Bashar got out of the helicopter while his tie was moving in the wind and entered the palace with his bodyguards. Kassim ran toward him.

"Beat those terrorists as hard as you can and clear Damascus. Can you do this?" Bashar asked the Iranian General.

"We have set a series of fighter jets to attack their base," Kassim replied. "They are under pressure on the earth and on the air. We'll search house to house in coming days in order to fully remove them."

"Don't have merci. Burn their corpses to remove even their smell from Damascus," Bashar said.

Al Nusra and Free Army were losing their forces around Damascus. There was the dead bodies of fighters and revolutionists all over the streets in the south of Damascus and the army was pushing back the invaders using air forces.

Nothing could be seen or heard from Abu Bakr's men. They had disappeared in Damascus and had hidden in the calm spots far from Damascus. After being failed in Sayyidah Zaynab Mosque and being tricked by Iranians, they had decided to set backward.

Abu Bakr's war tactic was this: "War in Damascus is like committing suicide. The Islamic state can announce its existence outside Damascus.

Abu Bakr ordered his men to shoot every outsider who leaves Damascus. He intended to dominate vital parts of Syria out of the control of the Syria government army.

So he dominated parts of Aleppo, Homs, Daraa, and all the Ar-Raqqah governorate and ordered his forces to kill any members of other rebel groups.

16

The bloody return of the monster

By involving more difficulties in the center of Damascus, al-Nusra and Free army fighters preferred to stay in Juber district in the east of Damascus waiting for another opportunity.

The disorganized cities of Syria were captured by Abu Bakr one after another and he established his government in these cities.

When Assad saved Damascus he felt revealed but the hard time and disaster had just begun for the people in other parts of Syria under the control of the Islamist Jihadi groups. People formed resistance cores in towns and villages. One of them, named "Ghosts" was formed by some young Syrians who attacked anonymously the fighters and killed them.

The ghosts had caused a lot of panic between the fighters. The ghosts jumped on fighters in a sudden and throttled them.

There was a rumor between the fighters that these are the ghosts of the killed citizens who have returned for revenge.

After announcing the Islamic State in Syria, Abu Bakr called high ranked commanders and governors of different cities in a very important meeting to explain them his plans for future. "I have told the recruitment sections to attract as many as possible jihadis," he told the governors.

"It was a very good decision to leave Damascus. Now we have an independent Islamic government," the governor of Ar-Raqqah said.

"There is no way that Iranians let Damascus fall. Al-Nusra and Free Syrian Army destructed themselves but the future Muslims Caliphate is ours," Abu Bakr said.

"We have secured all of our regions by side road bombs," a governor from the south of Aleppo said.

"We will destroy every annoying outsider fighters. There is no joke or compliment in the Islamic State," Abu Bakr said.

"With all these massacres I wonder if anyone outside the Syria would like to join us or not," Abu Hajar said in an anxious tone.

Abu Bakr reacted. "We have to bold the concept of heaven. The young full of passion only would be deceived by the dream of heaven," Abu Bakr said, "I remember we used to issue documents illustrating the conveyance of the lands in heaven to suicide bombers. There was a chaos among the young to go to heaven sooner."

***

The failed army of al-Nusra, led by Jolani was withdrawing from Damascus, exhausted and scattered. They had no more power and in this situation they were caught by forces of Abu Bakr and were slaughtered. There was a bloody battle where ever they entered. Jolani noticed his previous bases had been captured by Abu Bakr. He got so angry and sent a message in the draft box of Ayman al-Zawahiri. "The Iraqi evil pig had stepped into my shoes. I leave him alone because I don't want dirty my hands with his blood. But you must be more careful for your next choices," he wrote.

Jolani was wasting time. His tired defeated group was looking for a point to reinforce. But everywhere was under the control of Abu Bakr ant more fighting had no use, because it only would increase the casualties. Finally al-Nusra was stopped in some parts in Homs.

The forces of the Free Syrian Army almost had the same situation after being defeated in Damascus. They disintegrated. Some of them went to Turkey and some others started a secret life in hidden holes waiting for another chance for attack.

Abu Bakr was preparing some of his fresh military squads for a new battle. The fighters were being hardly trained. This time the target was Iraq. He send a representative to al-Anbar governorate to negotiate with the Sunni tribes for the vow of allegiance. Some Iraqi officers in charge of city security were also contacted. In return of a huge amount of money they guaranteed that they won't resist the entrance of the forces of Abu Bakr.

Iraq was the same as it was 1400 years ago. The tribes still existed and the primitive culture still had a special position in the society. The army officers would sell the city for a little amount of money. So the cities fell before any military conflict. Part of this inaptitude and irresponsibility was because of the governments. The city of Ramadi fell as easy as Ar-Raqqah in Syria.

Abu Bakr awarded some points in Syria to its governors and returned to Iraq, his homeland. He know Iraqis very well. The government of Iraq realized the disaster 24 hours after the fall of the cities. Abu Bakr started by his favorite hobby to frighten everyone. He ordered to place bombs in houses in 30 points in Baghdad and Samarra in Shiite districts and set the explosion clock on the midnight because Abu Bakr believed all the miseries happen in the midnight.

He also ordered to kidnap imams from different mosques in Baghdad. The head of kidnapped persons would be found in the waste bins.

"I'm so amazed that during our absence Iraq has calmed down and the number of suicide attacks has decreased," once Abu Bakr told Abu Hajar.

"There would be tens of suicide teams just if you want," Abu Hajar said.

"Gather the widows, derelict kids and faithful girls, Bring Mulla Osman Afghani to give them a speech about heaven," Abu Bakr said, "Prepare one thousand suicide vests, we are going to immerse Iraq in blood and fire."

Later he ordered to prepare throwing bombs to be thrown in the middle of government soldiers who might resist the fighters of the Islamic State. There were big scorpions to spread in the kafirs' house and the soldiers' residence and cause horror.

These bombs were thrown by devices like catapult in a very ridiculous and primitive way. The one who managed the device was a long bearded man from

Chechen who believed in his despicable act as a pray. He was told that all those scorpions would testify on doomsday that he was a faithful man so it would lead him more easily to paradise.

The scorpions bombs were thrown early in the morning before sunrise when everyone had slept. As the people of Iraq were used to the explosion sounds they wouldn't react, so the scorpions could went quietly toward their bait.

***

In a poor district in Ramadi, Iraq, the agents of the Islamic State pushed the women, girls and little kids in a bus. The women had borqa on their faces and the agents touched every part of their body that they could. They abused every woman and girl that they wanted. They even didn't let go the young fiancés. A boy who was passing through that district with his fiancé was beaten for having illegitimate relations. The boy resisted in front of them and swore back. The fighters got mad and fired a bullet inside his head. Then they brought his fiancé inside a house, attacked the poor girl and raped her. Then they pulled her inside the bus while she had passed out.

The bus moved toward a far point outside the city. The women hummed. When they descended the bus they were categorized into three groups: kids, women and young girls. Mulla Osman Afghani was supposed to speak separately for each of these groups.

Mulla was an expert of brain washing and he could lead everyone to a complete destruction by his words. "Wearing the suicide belts will survive your child from hunger and misery, it will lead you to paradise, it will bless your orphans. If you do not accept it you are going to be slaves for the fighters or you have to go to Syria to breastfeed the children of the women of Nikah." he said in his speech for women.

Now it was the young girls' turn. "Wearing the suicide vests has a great advantage for the virgins. Girls go directly, as fast as light, to the first circle of the heaven after the explosion. They must wait some moments here while the angels examine their virginity. If a girl isn't virgin, she stay 99 days at this point, till she is brought to higher circles," Mulla Osman told them

The girls were easily deceived by his bullshit and were eagerly fastening their suicide belts. "Good for the ones who are taken by handsome boys in heaven!" Mulla said when he saw their enthusiasm.

***

Abu Samareh an active member of the Islamic State in Europe and America had secretly arrived in Iraq by the invitation of Abu Bakr al-Baghdadi. Caliph had called him to consult him on solutions for fighter recruitment and invite the people around the world to join his caliphate. Abu Samareh was indeed a cyber crime prodigy on social networks, a real professional in deceiving.

He suggested to caliph that charming characters would attract lots of people toward the Islamic lands.

"What is your solution?" Abu Bakr asked him, "we want to have plenty of citizens and fighters in the territory of the Islamic caliphate."

Abu Samareh who had thought of his plans before, started. "We must think like a movie director," he told, "You attracted your men promising heaven. But I say, from now on, you have to present an ideal image of your government. For example the pictures of your fighters in figures like movie stars on the internet. I think of Hollywood techniques, you will see how girls and women would be attracted to these men and your caliphate."

"I want fighters. The girls and women are proper for the sexual jihad," Abu Bakr said.

"Let me be frank," Abu Samareh said, "When young Arabs and also non Arabs find sexual attraction and they discover a place where they can fight along with having relations with girls and women, they would be attracted quickly."

"I have read that it was the same during the Othman caliphate," the caliph said, "Their army was filled by girls and women and there was passion beside the war maps inside tents."

"You are also a caliph," Abu Samareh said, "It is better to follow the foretime. I am going to start. I am sure we will succeed."

Abu Samareh went to Abu Bakr's fighters to take pictures from them in different positions. Some of their faces were really unpleasant. But with special techniques Abu Samareh tried to show a warrior's attractive face. He filmed some fighters who were expert in beheading while coddling cats and dogs. He took pictures from beautiful slim women of Nikah while they had guns in their hands and borqa on their faces, showing their body curving under their clothes, standing among men.

Gradually, by spreading these pictures and clips in social networks, a wave of demand for joining the Islamic State raised. Plenty of immigrant Arab girls living in Europe fled to travel agencies to buy tickets to Turkey.

The jihadis cheated girls and women by promising marriage. In the funniest situation when a non-Arab Christian girls involved the jihadis' deception, the Arab jihadi suggested her to convert to Islam. "If you don't convert to Islam and you come here, you would be a sex slave who is permissible to everyone. But if you become a Muslim I promise you will only be mine," one of these Arabs had told a Christian girl.

In the next step Abu Samareh performed a new plan. A guy named "Zeynal" who had joined the Islamic State appeared in social networks looking like rock stars. This disgusting character with a long beard, shaved moustache and fashion t-shirts holding a Setar in his hands ached the hearts of many student girls in Malaysia. They contacted him on his page. "Get the ticket to Turkey immediately and come to Syria. I'm waiting you there," he said to girls.

The full veiled girls from Malaysia went to Hatay the border line in Turkey to reach Syria. But as soon as they arrived in the jihadists' camp they would understand what a big mistake they had made. Most of them were given to the fighters one after another or they were engaged in kitchen or bathrooms for cleaning.

The women were still the bait for jihadis. Abu Bakr equipped about thirty women who had volunteered for suicide attacks in Baghdad and Samarra. The women exploded themselves and they killed tens of Iraqis with them. Unlike the promise given to the suicide women their children instead of going to school and redemption, were given to the Salafi clergymen to be brainwashed and get ready for the next suicide attacks.

17

The city of women and bondwomen

The ambitious project of the caliph was getting
complete by focusing on Mosul and trying to add it to
the Islamic State. He sent one of his men named "Abu
Muslim Torkamani" as his secret agent to Mosul to
investigate the situation. Muslim started negotiation
with heads of some Sunni tribes to take their vow of
allegiance for Abu Bakr. The Sunnis in Mosul
welcomed Abu Bakr's agent warmly and told him
whatever they knew.

Muslim asked them about the time when money is
sent to banks for the salary of the employees by the
Kurdistan government and got the complete answers.
The tribe heads didn't suspect at all that they were
planning for a big burglary and they should not have

given such information to an stranger who they didn't knew properly.

Abu Muslim also gained some information about dams and oil wells and left Mosul after three days of wandering inside it.

Abu Bakr was waiting for fresh forces in order to start his operation to occupy Mosul. "You get your way to Mosul. The forces will arrive soon," Abu Samareh told him.

Caliph moved his scattered army with no hesitation and passed easily the cities of Iraq one after another and reached outside the Mosul.

Some Sunni tribes who didn't like the Shiite prime minister of Iraq were ready to welcome Abu Bakr's army. Abu Bakr hesitated a little behind the gates of Mosul to make sure that the government forces won't resist.

As soon as one of the spies inside the city reported that everything is set the caliph army invaded the city like insects on their armored vehicles. A few soldiers who weren't aware of anything started shooting who immediately got killed. The tribes who had made the allegiance vow to Abu Bakr, came to streets to celebrate the entrance his army. Everything was arranged from before and the responsible agents for dams, refineries and specific centers who had been assigned started their work with no trouble.

The first night of the city fall passed quietly. From the second night the exciting job of the fighters started. The caliph's soldiers started invasion to people's houses in groups. The operation was named "gaining bondwomen" which meant capturing women and girls to have sex with soldiers.

One night, the fighters went to the house of a tribe head to gain a bondwoman. There was a party inside the house which the fighters interrupted. "Give us any woman and girl you have inside the house," a soldier asked the tribe head, "our soldiers are single and they need a bed partner."

"What is this shameless suggestion? Get out of my house," The tribe head answered angrily.

The fighter hit him with his butt stock. The tribe head now could understand the depth of his stupidity. But he had no way out.

"Everyone should help the Islamic State. Your girls and women will help our soldiers to have focus and peace of mind," the young fighter said.

Some young girls and middle aged women were chosen between the guests who were screaming. The tribe head was being revenged for his fool support of Abu Bakr. And now the women of his tribe were paying the price.

In the coming days, there were big tables in some big squares of Mosul and some caliph's agents were inviting the young men of Mosul to be a part of the Islamic State and join the fighters.

The agents of the Islamic State patrolled in the streets and inside the stores to respond to any conflicts. Some clothing stores were attacked. The reason was the doll mannequins which seemed seductive to men. They put a black cloth on their head and body to consider the Islamic rules.

Every night after the prayer the caliph's agents had their dinner and went to different districts to do the "gaining bondwomen" operation. After 9 o'clock all the houses were in complete dark and a deathlike silence filled the city.

People locked the doors of their houses and spoke quietly in their homes to prevent their women or girls being stolen by agents. The houses which were taken unaware would surly lose their women.

Sometimes a door was knocked and no one opened it. The agents climbed the walls to enter the house or find a way in by breaking the windows. Sometimes the house was empty but if they caught the residents inside the house they even raped and tortured women and girls in front of the eyes of men. If men protested, they would be killed or hardly beaten.

By capturing about 150 women the fighters had the complete essential needs to meet their pleasure. The captive girls and women were sent from a soldier to another and if they objected they would be whipped. According the law stated by Abu Bakr, soldiers permitted to do whatever they wanted to these women and girls.

Whenever the soldiers were fed up by women their attitude changed direction toward the young boys. Some Salafi clergymen had allowed relations with boy kids. Because they had found in their book that there are beautiful boys in paradise so it was legal to have them in this world too.

Abu Bakr was thinking of making a second Raqqah in Mosul. He thought occupying some points in Iraq and Syria and joining them to each other would be enough for establishing an Islamic Emirate.

Abu Samareh had an attractive idea on the issue of captured women in Mosul. "If we show a more joyful atmosphere for the young people they will have more enthusiasm to join the Islamic State," He told Abu Bakr.

Abu Bakr was waiting the rest of his words. His idea was to operate a slave market of these women so a vast number of the young would be attracted to. He believed everyone would like to try the chance of multi partners.

"I have also concluded that the promise of heaven is not enough for the young. The heaven is here. Instead of going to the other world for sake of a few women, we can build them up a heaven here, in our Islamic Caliphate. The only condition to enjoy it is to swear allegiance to the Islam's caliph." Abu Bakr said.

The ridiculed Islamic Caliphate was turning into a big scandal. But there were nothing to worry about. By the time they can make a fatwa and there are fools who consider the fatwa as the rule of God, every impossible thing becomes possible.

Abu Bakr intended to make a charismatic face from himself to attract the hearts of the Muslims from all around the world. He wore the dress for clergyman, made his beard tidy and put on a black turban. His pictures were vastly tweeted and there were someone deceived and it was enough for the caliph.

Once Abu Samareh called Abu Bakr in the middle of the night to give him an interesting suggestion which had just came to his mind.

Abu Bakr asked him to explain his idea in a sleeping tone.

Abu Samareh went directly to his main issue. "I have worked on European girls, from both groups of Arab origin and European or American origin," he said.

-"OK. Where is the important part?"

-"They come to Iraq and Syria and return to their homes when they are pregnant. Their new born babies would be European or American while growing up in a fighter family. After a while they will occupy the country where they were raised and will join it to the Islamic State."

"We don't have lack of sperm for women in Iraq and Syria. But are you sure that the border security guards are so naïve that they would let these women easily enter USA or the countries in Europe?" Abu Bakr said.

"Right now some beautiful European girls are around me who say they are waiting impatiently to join the Islamic State and become pregnant sooner to give birth to brave fighters for jihad," Abu Samareh said.

"Are you sure European girls tend to be with you with this face of yours?" caliph said sarcastically.

"I have several children from these beauties who are the future fighters of the west world," Abu Samareh said.

"O.K. Do whatever is needed," Abu Bakr said, "But I really like to add the women from Iran in this project. Their country is the land of heresy. If we occupy there, we have done a very big jihad."

Abu Samareh got quiet for some seconds. "I have tried it," he said, "But there was no use. They won't be deceived by our promises. They hate us deep in their hearts and they don't like adventures which put them in danger."

Abu Bakr knitted his brows and said nothing more.

***

Domination over Mosul, Ar-Raqqah and some other cities in Iraq had made Abu Bakr proud of himself. He ordered to change the verses from surah al-kafirun. In this verses Quran says that every people can has his own religion.

Caliph believed this verse are in opposition with jihad for punishing kafirs. He sent his order to the governors in Ar-Raqqah, Mosul, Tikrit, Falluja and Daraa. A council formed in the Islamic State which acted as an advisory council. The members of this council were appointive and their duty was to decide about the ways of executing the laws of Sharia in the cities.

The advisory council formed a group named "al-Hasiba" which had the duty of enjoining the good and forbidding wrong. The members of this group patrolled in the city with whips and sentenced whoever who didn't have a proper hijab. Everyday plenty of people were whipped in the public. Once a man from Mosul dared to advise them about their behavior. It had bad consequences for him. The agents pulled his tongue out of his mouth and cut it by a sword.

***

The office of caliph in Mosul had received worrying news about the new born children of the women of Nikah in Tunisia which seemed rather terrifying. The security section of the Islamic state quickly sent some special agents to Tunisia to investigate the case. The agents went to some hospitals in the city to visit the women and their babies. There was a real disaster. The new born babies had horrible strange faces.

In the beginning it seemed to the agents that they had entered a zoo. A baby had a horrific horn of meat. The nose of another baby was deformed like a trunk which made breathing difficult for the baby. Another baby was roaring like an elephant.

The agents asked about the mothers. They were told that the mothers had ran away of the hospital after seeing their deformed babies.

They reported the situation to Abu Hajar. He rushed hotfoot to caliph. "The women of Nikah had given birth to zombies. There are only twelve healthy babies, other eleven ones are deformed," he said.

Caliph ordered to take good care of the healthy babies until they are grown up. The girls only needed to be nine years old to be married to the fighters of Islam and have children.

"Kill the deformed ones and if you could reach their mothers, rape them then kill them," Abu Bakr said.

He was completely sure these women had relations with other men after the soldiers of Islam and that is the reason their children are deformed. So they deserved death.

He had forgotten those poor women were abused by several soldiers in only one night and what painful disasters they have been through. Abu Hajar dared to mention this point. "Maybe multi intercourses in only one night has made this problem," he said.

Abu Bakr got angry. "Damn your poisonous and devil theories," he said, "No way! All the jihadis have pure sperms. It is the fault of the women."

Abu Hajar mentioned another difficult problem. Some of the mothers of healthy children had also ran away. So the babies are not fed properly.

"Among the suicide women, choose the most fattened ones with big breasts to feed the babies. Establish a nursery in Ar-Raqqah, take the feeding women there. Every woman who gives birth in Ar-Raqqah is charged to breastfeed three hours a day the babies other than her own baby," Abu Bakr suggested which was very weird.

"We can advertise on internet for recruiting breastfeeding women," Abu Hajar once again gave a stupid suggestion.

"This suggestion equals being mocked. So shut up and do what I said," Abu Bakr said decisively.

18

Whipping men, executioner women

The Islamic state had established patrols named religious guidance patrol who wandered like tramps in the streets and alleys of Mosul, Ar-Raqqah and some other districts. The masked agents screamed behind loudspeakers. "If there is anyone who hasn't yet sworn his allegiance vow, he must be aware that the flames of hell will be his share. Don't hesitate."

Some people gave up and vowed not to be killed. Everyone who made his vow of allegiance, was given a paper illustrating: "I put myself under the supervision of The Islam Caliph to be led to heaven by his intercession. He has all rights reserved over my life, my property and my honor." and the person should sign and finger the paper.

One of the petrol's actions was to identify and control the churches. The soldiers of caliph were allowed to rape the nuns inside the churches. In Mosul most of the Christians were locked in their houses and didn't dare to exit. Some churches were set on fire. If a Christian was caught he had to pay tribute and let the fighters to abuse their women and girls.

Abu Bakr had also ordered to terminate the activity of druids and wizards. Once a petrol identified the location of the fortune tellers. Some men were selling spells. They were thrown into the fire after being arrested to become an example for the others. The Islamic State agents arrested some men and women in cemeteries while burring some spell. By the order of the Judge upon Sharia the cemetery was determined unclean and they had to completely destroy it.

By starting of the month of Ramadan caliph increased his religious severity. There were big banners all over the town indicating, "We are responsible for your future in heaven or hell. Don't break your fast."

The Sharia police in Ar-Raqqah, Mosul and Aleppo had also forbidden eating for the patients, kids and disabled people. They believed that everyone should fast, with no exception. A thirteen year old boy was arrested while eating a biscuit and he was continuously whipped on his back. The judge of Sharia ordered to crucify the boy. A poor boy was also arrested on the day of Eid al-Fitr, when he had stolen a pair of shoes from the mosque, not to stay barefoot in the celebrating ceremony. He was sentenced to have his right hand cut off.

The Islamic State fans were active in different ways online. They wrote messages on social networks to attract young Muslims to Iraq and Syria. "The god decides who shall keep the flag of Jihad. No one merits for Jihad unless by God's will. When you decide to turn to us, it means that God has a special will for you. Good for you!"

There were clips tweeted over the social networks showing the devises of jihadists in a sentimental way. In these videos an ugly mufti appeared on the screen.

"In Islam nothing is more precious than putting horror in the hearts of kafirs," he said.

He then taught the method of making a hand-made bomb and how to place it in houses or cars of the kafirs.

One day Abu Bakr who wasn't feeling good called Abu Hajar and told him about his foolish decision which was far from a caliph's dignity. "Tell all the fighters to gather their urine in big cans. Then have someone shed all that urine in the Tigris river. Also prepare oil from refinery to infect water in Tigris," he said.

"But why should we do this?" Abu Hajar asked.

"I want a mess in Baghdad and the Saladin governorate. When people don't have any water to drink, then they have to drink from the urine of our soldiers and they will find tendency toward us," Abu Bakr said.

"It's kind of a shameless magic," Abu Hajar said.

"We will mesmerize them to accept our caliphate," Abu Bakr said justifying himself.

"We have arrested some Jew druids in Mosul. If you order I will ask them to make a more effective mixture and shed in water," Abu Hajar said.

"The Jews are phonies. They may do something which has an opposite effect. Use urine and oil," Abu Bakr said.

***

By increasing the activities of the Islamic State in Ar-Raqqah, Mosul and parts of Aleppo, Special courts were established who had duty of making the kafirs to repent beside of issuing criminal statutes. People had to attend the courts weekly to confess in order to remove their sins.

There was always long queues. "Did you eat fast food? Did you watch football games? Did you smoke? Did you think of women or did you masturbate?" These were the questions asked by the person in charge of repenting.

Some times when the sins were many, they sent the guilty one to special court to be sentenced by whipping. They believed the blood caused by the lashes would purify the soul. The whipped person also had to pay an amount of money as the purifying charge.

Beside all the night patrols were carried out. A night some masked agents entered a coffee shop in Mosul where some young people were drinking and watching football. The agents attacked them and kicked their tables down. A fighter shot the TV. They brought the lashes out of their pockets and tied the hands of the young guys and made them lay on the ground.

"Don't you know it's forbidden to watch football matches in Islam?" an agent with a Pakistani accent said.

Another fighter was whipping them mercilessly. A young boy screamed and said a dirty word in English.

"Better be sure than sorry!" the unwise fighter told who couldn't understand any of his words.

After beating them, the agents gave the young men a subpoena to attend the court the day after. They shouldn't cleanse the blood residue in order to be checked by the judge and be determined if the poison of the sin had left their body or not. If not they should repeat the whipping.

Whipping and making people to repent was the usual plan of the city patrolling. One day, a young woman was arrested by two Arab women of a British nationality because wearing a burqa which wasn't thick enough to cover her face.

The guilty women were brought to a judge of Sharia. "Crazy woman! Don't you know here is a the Islamic State? Why are you so shameless?" The judge told her after admitting her crime.

He wrote something on a paper. "You can choose the method of your punishment," he told the woman, "Do you want 70 lashes or being bitten?"

The woman who had witnessed horrible scenes of being whipped, got so happy and chose to be bitten. She was relieved of escaping a hard punishment.

The judge called the executive agent who was an Arab woman. The guilty woman was more relieved when she saw her making sure that a woman jaw wouldn't hurt that much.

"Bite her wrists," the judge told the woman.

The executioner came forward and the guilty woman brought out her hand. The woman started biting. It was so hard that the guilty woman started screaming.

Suddenly the blood sprayed out. The judge stood up and looked the scene carefully. The sharp teeth of the executioner had cut the woman's artery and she had fainted.

The executive woman indifferently cleaned the blood around her mouth by her sleeve and swallowed the rest. "She didn't survive. It's not my fault," she told the judge apathetically.

"I should remember to give you the beheading cases the next time," the judge said while laughing viciously.

The situation was frustrating and unbearable in the districts under the control of the Islamic State. Nevertheless their propaganda of the Islamic State on the internet was encouraging people around the world to join them. "Do you want the heaven? Don't hesitate, the gate is here," They said.

There was even an image of their heaven passport in the social networks and it was insisted that anyone who joins the Islamic State would instantly gain a heaven passport.

Abu Bakr al-Baghdadi received brief reports from the districts under his domination. He was satisfied with the procedure of implementing the Islamic ruling and punishing the people. He was thankful to God.

"The world is proud of itself to be under the shadow of such a caliph," once Abu Hajar told him who was following him everywhere.

"God knows I do nothing but his orders and the orders of Mohammad our prophet," he replied bringing Abu Hajar into account for just once.

"You are the medium to take people to heaven," Abu Hajar added who had used to confirm all the bullshit from the caliph, "One day everyone would understand that the only way to heaven is to be allegiant to you."

There was a wedding in a rather cool evening in a wealthy quarter of the city Mosul in the Nineveh Province. The "Enjoining good and forbidding wrong Patrol" who had always been waiting for an excuse to struggle with people noticed the wedding car and the cars following it. A group of the armed agents with masked faces got close to the cars for an investigation.

A fighter from Aljazeera went toward the wedding car. "You didn't observe the Islamic rules," he told the groom.

The agents noticed the bride who had a nice bridal veil. Her low-necked dress attracted his attention. He moved toward the bride.

"Where do you go asshole? I'm standing just here," the groom yelled.

The other agent went toward the groom, got him out of the car, opened his tie and undressed him.

A man with beards arrived and went to the bride. The other agents smiled. The groom in that situation with only one underwear ran to his wife to rescue her. The poor man knew that in some seconds they would rape his wife in front of his eyes. At the moment the man from Aljazeera shoot the groom and he fell on the ground.

After seeing this scene the woman lost her control and fisted and kicked the agents. She hit a fighter in face while she had hold a fighter's beard.

Another agent arrived and hold her arm and tried to push her to an unknown place. She dug her nails in his eyes. The soldiers of the caliph gave their second casualty. The fighters who understood it is useless to try to control her, shot and killed her. The angry agents didn't have pity for the dead body of the woman and brought it to a corner to rape it in group.

The ministry of Sharia made a new story every day. One of their weird instructions was to make the uniform of the students and employees alike. Abu Bakr ordered everyone to wear similar Afghani and Pakistani clothing and forbid wearing jeans and t-shirts.

The Pakistani clothing was a long white dress. After this order all other clothes were collected from stores. Women also had to be wrapped in burqa.

There was a unisex system in the universities and the boys weren't allowed to be mixed with girls and study by their sides. Abu Bakr had commented that gender segregation would increase the students attention and focus on their lessons.

Abu Hajar showed the caliph a short film from a mixed student social camp which was found in an attack to a university. The freedom of relations between boys and girls made the caliph so angry that he ordered to Islamize the universities and separate boys and girls. The universities in Mosul and Ar-Raqqah were closed for some months in order to make modifications. Abu Bakr ordered all the professors and teachers to pass a religious coarse and the ones without beliefs were fired.

The women had the most difficult situation in the Islamic State. Two female squads named "Al-Khansaa" and "Umm al-Rayan" were established by caliph who managed the women affairs. These squads held kiosks in the crowded squares of town which recruited passing girls and women to marry the soldiers of the caliphate. They had made brochures with an statement on it: "Marrying to the soldiers of caliphate equals going to heaven."

Though women weren't allowed to go in the streets without Hijab and Burqa, but the anti vice office who worked under the supervision of the ministry of Sharia would send the girls arrested for not fully implementing the law, to military brigades to serve as a sex slave or do the cooking or cleaning services.

This punishment sometimes included also the foreign women who joined the caliphate state. As an example some girls and women from Malaysia and England who had met the fighters in the social networks and agreed on getting married and joining the Islamic State, started their works in the bathrooms and kitchens as soon as they arrived in Iraq and Syria. They were told giving any services to the soldiers is a Fardh.

An Australian girl who had arranged to get married to an Arab, escaped her home without informing her parents and she left for Syria.

As soon as she arrived in Syria and she entered Aleppo she was shocked by seeing the face of his beloved young man and decided to return. The ugly man who had became mad by her reaction raped her for several times and then introduced her to the service department to clean the toilettes and also work as a sex slave.

Sometimes there were also many ridiculous cases. For example an Arab fighter met a girl from Malaysia on the net and could communicate her with a faulty English language. The girl finally went to Syria and married him. The funny point was that the couple couldn't understand each other and they had to use a dictionary in order to be able to communicate to each other.

There was a funny and painful situation in the lands under the domination of Abu Bakr and everyone was caught there, he would have a miserable life. In Mosul a woman went to a store to buy a juice. When the woman pulled over her burqa to put the drinking straw in her mouth suddenly a group of the agents in charge of Enjoining Good and Forbidding Wrong arrived and started beating the woman in face. As usual in such situations the husband wouldn't stay indifferent. When her husband was trying to stop them, they attacked him in a big group and bludgeoned him too.

Once a few number of the soldiers from Assad army were caught by the members of the Islamic State. The agent brought the helpless soldiers into the main square of the city and asked people to feast and kick them. People attacked the soldiers in fear of being punished and beat them do death.

19

The women who end up in slave market

Abu Bakr was satisfied with the situation and he was
thinking that he is implying the Islam regulations. He
was planning another attack, so he sent the
commanders under his mandate a secret
announcement. He intended to move north to purge
Yazidis from an area settled by Kurds who weren't
Muslim. To create horror amongst the Yazidi people
he surrounded the city for several months. Though all
the escaping ways were blockaded, a few people
could hardly abandon their homes and reach the
mountains to survive the caliph's murderers.

People looked out of their windows frightened. They
could see black-wearing men holding flags with an
Arabic phrase on it. The big escape started and the
peasants rushed to the mountains. The caliphate

division hadn't entered the village yet. But some men in black arrived sooner in order to manage things. The horrified people escaped their houses with their undershirt even barefooted. Everything was confusing.

The moment arrived and the army of the caliph entered the village to start the plunder. They invaded the houses and killed whoever hadn't ran away yet. They first divided the girls and women from other family members. All the men who had stayed in the village had been massacred. A headsman queued all the men of the village and behead them by sword.

The caliph's soldiers said the house owners that the beautiful women are prior. The women inside the houses blackened their faces by coal if they had time to look more ugly. Some fighters made the girls to wash their faces. The women were caught and the fighters were cheerful.

A group of the fighters got the mission to follow the runaways. Some of the Yazidis had escaped on their cars and when they arrived to mountains they left their cars behind and parked them in a way to blockade the fighters' way. During this time women, kids and old men had more chance to go higher and safer in the mountain.

It was very hot during the day and the runaways had a very hard situation. They all used the same glass for drinking and the food was served in common dishes and they should eat with common spoons or by hand. Some scared pregnant women gave birth to their babies sooner or they aborted their fetus.

The fighter had reached the top of the mountain chasing the Yazidis. The old and the kids couldn't go any higher. It was a catastrophic tragedy. They died in front of everyone. Their water supply was running out.

An old woman was being carried by her son. She noticed the agony her son was bearing to carry her. She asked her son to put her down to have a rest for some seconds. As soon as the son put her down, the old woman threw herself off the mountain. She couldn't stand her son's pain anymore.

A little further away a young woman had put her two children who had died of thirst in front of her and she was just staring at them without blinking.

Wherever the caliph's fighter arrived, they captured woman and killed the men if they were caught.

The captive women were brought down of the mountain and taken to stables. Some beautiful girls were chosen to be slaves for Abu Bakr and the others stayed in the stable. The avid soldiers of caliph had prepared a timetable to rape those women. The fighters went inside the stable during the nights and did whatever they wanted.

The women's food was a piece of dry molded bread with a bucket of water. The soldiers believed they deserve every torment because of their pagan religion. So they mixed some livestock urine in their drinking water.

They continued raping the captive women until some of them died of bleeding.

It was the caliph's order: Before the dooms day the slavery tradition must be vitalized. He had jumped centuries back in the history. He wanted the nice-eyed women to be sold more expensive. His suggested price was 170 dollars for beautiful women, 120 dollars for ordinary women and 80 dollars for the ugly ones.

One day Abu Bakr came to stable in a disguise and masked face to check the captive women. He touched the women. Caliph ordered everyone to leave the stable but his one guard in order to be able to do whatever he likes. After exiting the stable he ordered to feed the women properly because he found some of them very thin and weak. He wanted them fattened. Getting close to them was also forbidden.

A day prior to taking the women to slave market, some female agents of the Islamic State had the mission to take the captive women from stable to a bathhouse to make them clean so they can be sold on a better price. The bathhouse was in the training camp. A Yazidi woman who had been raped multiple times had taken a sharp trenchant tool into the bathhouse with herself. The agents took them inside one by one and they had three minutes of time to wash and exit. After the delay of one of the women the agents suspected and started action. They saw blood exiting from one of the baths. When the agents arrived there, they saw the half alive body of a woman who had cut her vein. The nightmare of being sold in a slave market was even worse than being raped.

On a hot Tuesday, the slave market was set to be held in the Nineveh governorate. It was a rather long distance from the stable to the place of slave market. The women had been moved in a desert hot path with shackle and chain on their hands. Three robust agent of the caliph were accompanying the women and sometimes they whipped the women who moved slow to make them move faster.

They reached the market before noon. There was a huge banner in the slave market stating: "Revival of the forgotten tradition of women slavery."

The women were brought on the stage each of them holding a piece of paper on their necks. Arab men with thick moustaches and horrible faces were looking for good looking women. Some others were interested in the fattest.

"Are they obedient? Aren't they restive?" one of them asked.

"They are docile. If they don't obey they will do easily after a small punishment," the seller replied.

A young man had came from Baghdad. He was telling that it would be more cheap to buy a slave instead of going to the most low level brothels in Baghdad. He quickly picked an adorable slave for 170 dollars.

Among the crowd there was a Yazidi man who had survived miraculously. He saw his fiancée among the slaves. But he had no money to buy her. The women were being sold rapidly and the young Yazidi man was going here and there to find a way to buy his fiancée while looking at her who had stared at him. "Don't you have any money to buy you a slave?" a Kurd man who had noticed the impatience of the boy asked him.

The boy was silent in shame and embarrassment. The Kurd man brought 120 bucks out. "Which one do you want?" he asked him.

He pointed his fiancée. The Kurd man went to the seller. "I have chosen one. But I only have 120 bucks." he told the seller.

The seller looked at him and noticed a ring he was wearing. "It would be alright if you add it too."

The man accepted and the slave girl was bought and ran to her fiancé. The Kurd man accompanied the boy and the girl to his house in order to make them to escape in an opportunity to a safe district and get married to each other.

***

One day Abu Adnan the Treasury responsible of the Islamic State were called. "We want to start the coinage of the official Islamic State money and you are in charge of this job." Abu Bakr told him.

"It's a good idea. We can spread it to all Islamic countries and make it the united currency of Islam," Adnan said.

Abu Bakr took his history book and turned some pages. "1400 years ago and at the time of the Islam prophet, they used gold and silver. Our money is named Dinar and it's your responsibility to gather the needed gold and silver," he said.

"I command the soldiers to go to the houses of people and seize their jewelry," Adnan added.

Experienced squads were sent to mission to the wealthy districts of the city. They trespassed the houses and asked the owners to bring whatever gold and silver they had. If anyone resisted they'd searched the house by force and would kill the owner if they found any jewelry.

Caliph's men also rubbed some jewelry stores and stole the gold. They finally accused the robbers in the city. There were many jewelry store owners in police departments to complain against the robberies. "We'll survey the case," the agents of the Islamic State replied them.

There were so many similar ideas. Another idea which suddenly came to Abu Bakr's mind was to trade the corpses. He called Abu Samareh to benefit his criminal methods. "Do you know that we have numerous corpses under the ruins while their viscera is precious," Caliph told him, "Can you arrange the smugglers to negotiate with us?"

"I know some guys," Abu Samareh replied, "I'll take care of it."

Abu Bakr ordered to buy huge refrigerators to keep the corpses fresh inside them. By the caliph's order the dead no longer were abandoned and their bodies were taken to these fridges.

He called Abu Hajar to listen to his last report of the corpses and dead bodies. "What do you do with the bodies of killed people right now?" he asked him.

As usual Abu Hajar was trying to satisfy his boss. "I have told the commanders to put the bodies in front of wild dogs to be torn apart by animals. So the enemies would understand what is the destiny of the opponents," he said.

"Change that decision immediately," Abu Bakr said, "Tell all he commanders to gather the dead bodies and store them in the huge refrigeration units we have bought."

"And sell the meat to people later?" he said thinking that it all was a joke.

"Their body parts costs a lot, you idiot!" caliph said.

***

20

The last scene in inferno

There was a deep silence in the kingdom of the God. An angel's fly could be heard once in a while. Some painful voices could be heard a little further.

The angel who had left the rebel fighter in Aleppo was called to the court of God. He inspected some horrible dungeons on his way. There were several sinful people in these dark narrow corridors waiting for their doom. There were people among them who had waited for 48 thousands of years for their sentence to be determined.

angel entered the court. He was commanded to land in Syria and bring the rebel back. It seemed that his malevolent existence had spread the evil in that region.

Before being sent to this mission the angel was bound to bring some fools who had done suicide attacks from limbo to inferno. "Shouldn't they wait till the doomsday?" The angel asked.

"Replace them thousands of milestones away from inferno," he was ordered.

The angel flied toward the limbo. The suicide attackers were standing around a well with a bucket above it, in a hot draughty desert. They ate stinky planets once in a while.

They had horrible faces. It seemed that the parts of their faces were glued after destruction which gave them a patchy disgusting face.

The miserable hellish guys dropped the bucket into the well to quench their thirst. But when they raised it, they found a sludgy stinky water. But they drank it voraciously.

angel approached them. "There is an angel coming to us," one of them told the others.

They were still waiting for the nymphs they were promised. The angel threw a big metal net over them. They were all trapped. The net impact was so hard that some of their body parts fell around.

The angels carried the net along with those individuals in the sky. They were groaning. After a short distance they felt a warm wind blowing on their faces. The angel continued its flight like a giant airplane carefully and confidently. They felt more heat on top of a lake of lava and moaned in agony. The angel got closer to the lake. They suddenly witnessed a horrible scene. There were suspended hanging houses on top of the sea where people lived in. "What are those houses?" one of the suicide bombers asked in fear.

"They are the residency for people who deceived others in the name of religion. They must stay here till doomsday," the angel explained.

The suicide bombers who were getting to understand what they had done in the world saw familiar faces whom they knew their leaders in the world. Osama had sat near his suspended house, sorrowful, head between his knees. The whale who had swallowed him in the world was wandering around to continuously remind him of his catastrophic destiny.

A little further away Abu Masab had sat on his fire house like mesmerized creatures. The bombers were panicked. They saw houses with no resident. "Who are the owners of those empty houses?" one of them asked.

"They are the residency for people who gave fatwas in the name of God to mislead poor people." The angel replied.

The heat still increased. The temperature felt like one thousand degrees. They were getting close to about one thousand milestones from inferno. The angel considered some other agents were spreading some parts around hell. They finally landed in a swampy region. They felt like drowning in the ground but they could survive easily but started to sink in another point.

The angel departed toward the earth to bring the rebel previously landed in Aleppo. When he approached him he noticed his eyes were red in crying. The angel was ordered to abandon him in a desert where is neither cold nor hot until the final decision.

***

In the late evening of an autumn day, one of the men in charge of planning military operations for the Islamic State went to caliph. The meeting was secret and before it started an Arab fighter investigated the room with a pipe-like tool to make sure there is not any wiring device. There was a section in Islamic State named "Misleading Tricks center" which allowed every kind of dirty lies to proceed their aims.

The one in charge of this section was an ugly Mufti named Sheikh Telkut whose fatwas were sometimes mocked by people. He was the same guy who had forbidden women to touch carrots or cucumbers. Upon his order no grocery store was allowed to sell these two products to women.

He was mentioned as the thinking brain of that killer population who created new ideas from analyzing young Arab fighters' plans and ideas. One of his fool ideas was to capture Rome. Telkut installed a very big map sized 15*20 meters on the wall which showed the situation of the most countries in the world when he was giving the details of his idea to Abu Bakr. "Do you understand what I mean by Rome?" he told the caliph.

"Yes, All the today Europe," Abu Bakr said.

"We are going to occupy them in the future. Iran is also the same Rome 14 centuries ago which will be finally defeated by us," he continued.

"What about the USA?" caliph asked.

"Some of the states will fall rapidly by Muslims and other states gradually will make their vow of allegiance with the Islamic Caliphate," Telkut replied rapidly.

Abu Bakr had a disgusting smile on his face. He was thinking of a clear tomorrow but remembering Kobani females fighters who were killing his men kept on teasing him. He suddenly changed the subject. "Kurdish women are killing our soldiers in Kobani to prevent them from going to heaven. What do you think of it?" he asked Telkut.

"It is superstition," Telkut said, "Being killed by a woman doesn't count at all."

He made a fatwa at the moment, "If a woman kills a fighter, one hundred of women will be given to killed jihadi in paradise. Put it in your men's head."

Some days later the Islamic States Think Tank in Ar-Raqqah received reports about finding documents in an industrial university of technology in Mosul which demonstrated vast scientific research on using uranium in making weapons of mass destruction.

The caliph was reported and he consulted Abu Samareh. As usual Abu Samareh said nothing but promising words. He insisted having a bomb is not enough for them if they want to rule the word.

"The Islamic State must be equipped. We must save for a rainy day. The apocalypse happens when we intend it. We will capture the whole world but the final battle takes place here," caliph said.

He immediately went to his note book to review his notes. "Columns of Devil soldiers in The land of Levant will tumble like melted walls when the major nuclear battle starts. No one is capable of confronting us on that day," Abu Bakr said.

The End

* 9 7 8 1 9 3 9 1 2 3 0 9 1 *